ACPL ITEM
DISCARDED

3 1833 00276 8221

P9-DTL-541

6·2·78

WHERE TO FIND MORE:

A Handbook to Reference Service

by

JAMES M. HILLARD

The Scarecrow Press, Inc.
Metuchen, N.J.   1977

Library of Congress Cataloging in Publication Data

Hillard, James M   1920-
   Where to find more.

   Supplements the author's Where to find what.
   1. Reference books--Bibliography. I. Hillard,
James M., 1920-   Where to find what. II. Title.
Z1035.1.H53   011'.02   77-6406
ISBN 0-8108-1039-5

Copyright © 1977 by James M. Hillard

Manufactured in the United States of America

TABLE OF CONTENTS

2007648

INTRODUCTION

There is perhaps no greater thrill for a librarian than to see a book of his own in print and to see a Library of Congress card for that book. In 1975, I wrote a modest little volume entitled Where to Find What which was intended to provide the harried reference librarian, particularly the one just beginning, with a ready source from which to start his or her own search for information. The book was not supposed to rival either Winchell or Shores, and of course it did not. I am happy to say, however, that its acceptance was far greater than either the publisher or I thought possible, and even more gratifying than the sales were the letters of appreciation from reference librarians in all sorts of libraries. The acclaim by reviewers, though, was less than enthusiastic--perhaps because they expected something that was neither promised nor intended. Nevertheless, the acceptance was so great that the publisher asked me to prepare a supplement and an updating of the original, and as far as possible to correct some of the deficiencies cited by reviewers. This I have attempted to do. I hope that the current volume, used in conjunction with Where to Find What, will help additional neophyte reference librarians in their service to library users.

The objective of this book is to add subject headings which were omitted from the first book, and also to list some newer titles for subject headings which were included in the earlier book. Subject headings which are repeated here from the first book are marked with an asterisk, and for these subjects users are advised to consult both volumes. This book is definitely a support and supplementary effort and should be regarded as such.

Although every effort was made in Where to Find What to list only items currently in print, some titles in the earlier book are already o. p. ; wherever this is the case, I have tried to supply newer titles in this volume.

There were some demurrers concerning my decision to include only in-print titles but since one use to which these books may be put is as a purchasing guide, I still feel that this is a valid decision. There were also some questions raised about the choice of subject headings in the first book. These were selected with the help of a panel of outstanding reference personnel and, while they do not conform to any designated list, they are, in my opinion, appropriate for a book of this type.

Grateful acknowledgment is given to the many reference persons who have used the first book and contributed suggestions for new subjects to be included in this volume. Not all subjects suggested were included. For example, one person asked for a comprehensive listing of postage rates by country and by period. This is just not something that one can find readily in one source. Scott's Catalogue will provide it if one wants to work that long and hard, but there is no easy answer for such a question. I have, however, tried to put in answers to most of the questions which were sent to me.

Acknowledgment and continued thanks are given to my secretary, Mrs. Catharine B. North, not only for her excellent proof reading, typing and general good work but also for assiduously checking ISBN numbers and prodding me to make sure I finished what I started.

JAMES M. HILLARD
Librarian
The Citadel
Charleston, S.C. 29409

December 31, 1976

SUBJECT HEADINGS USED

ACADEMIES
  see SERVICE ACADEMIES
ACOUSTICS
*ACTORS AND ACTRESSES
ACUPUNCTURE
AIR POWER
  see ARMED FORCES
*AIRCRAFT
  see also ARMED FORCES
AIRCRAFT - CIVIL
AMERICAN REVOLUTION
  see UNITED STATES HIS-
  TORY - REVOLUTION
*ANNIVERSARIES
  see HOLIDAYS
*ANTHROPOLOGY
*ANTIQUES
*AQUARIUMS
  see TROPICAL FISH
ARCHEOLOGY
*ARMED FORCES
*ARMS AND ARMOR
*ASTROLOGY
*ASTRONOMY
*AUTHORS
*AUTOGRAPHS
*AUTOMOBILES
AVIATION

BABY SITTING
*BALLET
BANKRUPTCY
BARTENDING

*BATTLES
BATTLESHIPS
  see SHIPS
BEES AND BEEKEEPING
*BIBLE
BIBLIOGRAPHY
*BIOGRAPHY
*BIRDS
BIRTH CERTIFICATES
*BLACKS
*BOATS AND BOATING
*BOOK PRICES
*BOOK REVIEWS
BOOKS - BANNED
*BOOKS - PLOTS AND CHAR-
  ACTERS
*BOXING
BRAND NAMES
BUDGET, PERSONAL
  see PERSONAL FINANCE
BUTTERFLIES

CALCULATORS
CALORIES
  see FOOD
CENSORSHIP
  see BOOKS - BANNED
CERAMICS
CHARACTERS IN LITERA-
  TURE
  see BOOKS - PLOTS AND
  CHARACTERS
*CHRONOLOGY

---

*Subject headings marked with an asterisk also appeared in
Where to Find What.

ix

see LANGUAGES, INTER-
NATIONAL
INTERNATIONAL STAND-
ARD BOOK NUMBERS
INTERNATIONAL STAND-
ARD SERIAL NUMBERS
*INVENTIONS

*JEWISH PEOPLE
JOURNALISTS

*KINGS AND RULERS
KNIVES
*KNOTS

*LABOR AND LABOR UN-
IONS
LANGUAGE, ARTIFICIAL
see LANGUAGE, INTER-
NATIONAL
LANGUAGE, INTERNATION-
AL
LAST WORDS
LAW ENFORCEMENT
LAWNS
LEGAL TERMS
LEGISLATION
*LITERATURE
LOTTERIES

MACHINE TOOLS
see POWER TOOLS
*MAGIC
*MAPS
see UNITED STATES -
ATLASES; RELIGION -
ATLASES
MEDICAL PROFESSION
MEDICARE
*METRIC SYSTEM
MILITARY LEADERS
*MINERALOGY
MISSIONS
MORTGAGE
MOTHS
MOTOR VEHICLE REGIS-
TRATION

*MUSEUMS
MUSHROOMS
*MUSIC AND MUSICIANS
MUSIC - COUNTRY AND
WESTERN
MUSICAL INSTRUMENTS
MYSTICISM

NAMES, GEOGRAPHIC
see GEOGRAPHY
NAMES, PERSONAL
NATIONAL ANTHEMS
NATURAL RESOURCES
NEWSPAPERMEN
see JOURNALISTS

OCEANS
*OPERA
OPPOSITE MEANING
see REVERSE DICTIONARY

PAINT AND PAINTING
PALMISTRY
PAPER
PARKS - NATIONAL
PARKS - STATE
PENSIONS
see RETIREMENT
PERIODICALS - INDICES
*PERSONAL FINANCES
PHARMACY
PHILANTHROPY
PHYSICS
PIRATES
*PLACE NAMES
see GEOGRAPHY
*PLANTS
PLAYING CARDS
*POETRY
see LITERATURE
*POLICE
*POLITICAL PARTIES
POLITICS
POLLUTION
*PORTS
see CITIES
POSTAL SERVICE

WHERE TO FIND MORE

ACADEMIES
see
SERVICE ACADEMIES

ACOUSTICS

For the mechanical or physical explanations of acoustics, one can turn to textbooks on the subject or handbooks in the fields of physics or electrical engineering. Most of the questions in the small or medium-sized library, however, will be concerned with acoustics in the home or small room. For a good discussion of the problems involved here, there are two good recent books.

Acoustic Techniques for Home and Studio, by F. Alton Everest. TAB Books, 1973. (ISBN 0-8306-2646-8)

Underlying Concepts of Room Acoustical Control--for the Intelligent Layman, by Jordan Levenson. Levenson Press, 1974. (ISBN 0-914442-05-8)

ACTORS AND ACTRESSES*

Who Was Who on Screen, by Evelyn Mack Truitt. Bowker, 1974. (ISBN 0-8352-0719-6)
This lists over 6000 actors and actresses who died between the years 1920 and 1970. A sincere attempt is made to list every film credit for each person listed as well as such vital statistics as dates of birth and death, marriages,

children. The listings are complete, containing not only the movies in which the biographee starred but every known film appearance, whether as an extra or in a selected short subject. It is a valuable addition to any library which receives questions on the history of the film, but perhaps is not as complete in its listings as the two-volume Scarecrow Press publication, Forty Years of Screen Credits, which was listed in Where to Find What.

ACUPUNCTURE

Increasing interest in the practice of acupuncture is creating more library questions about what it is and what it actually does. The following book will be helpful in explaining the practice but should be distributed with care. The uninitiated should be advised not to attempt to practice on themselves (or anyone else!).

Complete Guide to Acupuncture, by Masaru Toguchi. Frederick Fell, 1974. (ISBN 0-8119-0240-4)
This book is written by a current practitioner of the art of acupuncture and is intended to give the reader a history of the subject as well as an introduction to the terminology used and to beliefs behind the scientific aspects of the practice. The book is arranged by parts of the body, with a full discussion of the diseases or medical disorders which may attack each part. The diseases discussed cover a wide range, from insomnia to chest colds, and there are many diagrams and charts which explain which regions will be helped by which treatment. In addition to acupuncture, the ancient science of Moxacautery is also discussed. This is the placing of flammable material on the skin and lighting it to counteract the disease.

AIR POWER
see
ARMED FORCES

AIRCRAFT*
see also
ARMED FORCES*

Encyclopedia of Air Warfare, by Christopher Chant.   Crowell,
    1976.   (ISBN 0-690-00606-3)
        This book is excellent for profile drawings of military
aircraft and for technical specifications of the leading planes
over the years.   It is excellent for the evolution of the use
of airpower in wartime situations and is good for history of
the effect of airpower on ground operations.

Military Aircraft of the World, by John W. R. Taylor and
    Gordon Swansborough.   Rev. ed.   Scribner's, 1976.
    (ISBN 0-684-14398-4)
        This is a revised edition of a standard work in the
field of military aircraft and is excellent for technical specifications as well as individual aircraft identification by sil-
houette or photograph.   Since it is a relatively inexpensive
purchase, it should be in any library where there is extensive interest in either aircraft or military aviation.

AIRCRAFT - CIVIL*

Census of U.S. Civil Aircraft, ed. by Sylvia Goring.   U.S.
    Federal Aviation Agency.   Government Printing Office.
    Annual since 1965.
        A census of all aircraft registered in the United
States.   It lists each one by number, manufacturer, make,
model and type, and the type of use for which it is regis-
tered.

Civil Aircraft of the World, by John W. Taylor.   Rev. ed.
    Scribner's, 1975.   (ISBN 0-684-14134-5)
        The books listed in Where to Find What were almost
all, with the exception of Janes, restricted to military aircraft.   This book discusses civil aircraft from the very
smallest to the SST and gives specifications concerning
weight, payload, passengers, engines, etc.   Each entry is
accompanied by an excellent photograph.   Use is necessarily
by means of an index, since planes are arranged by manufacturer rather than by name.

AMERICAN REVOLUTION
see
UNITED STATES HISTORY - REVOLUTION

ANNIVERSARIES
see
HOLIDAYS

ANTHROPOLOGY*

Dictionary of Anthropology, by Charles Wenick. Littlefield-
Adams, 1970. (Reprint of 1956 ed.) (ISBN 0-8371-
2094-2)
Over 10,000 entries on all aspects of anthropology,
including archeology, linguistics, physical and cultural anthropology. Reliable because of its dependence upon the
pioneers and leaders of the field for information.

ANTIQUES*

Basic Book of Antiques, by George Michael. Arco, 1974.
(ISBN 0-668-03433-8)
This is intended for the beginning collector of antiques
and has chapters on each of the many varieties of antiques
which can be collected. The first chapter, a good summary
of what the book hopes to accomplish, is called "How to col-
lect and enjoy antiques." Each succeeding chapter deals with
a specific type of antique and helps one to identify and price
various items. Particularly valuable for the beginner are
the glossary at the end of each chapter, an excellent bibliography and a good index.

How to Know American Antique Furniture, by Robert Bishop.
Dutton, 1973. (ISBN 0-525-47337-8)
This is an excellent guide for the beginning antique
collector but is useful to the old hand as well. It is well
illustrated with both photographs and line drawings to help
the user identify special characteristics of each period of
American furniture. It is arranged by period, from the
earliest to the latest, and has an excellent index.

The Kovel's Complete Antiques Price List: A Guide to the
1974-1975 Market for Professionals, Dealers and Collectors, edited by Ralph and Terry Kovel. Crown, 1974.
(ISBN 0-517-516772)

This is an annual publication which lists all known
selling prices of various antiques during the past year. Almost 50, 000 items are listed and priced.

AQUARIUMS*
see
TROPICAL FISH

ARCHEOLOGY

Guide to Cretan Antiquities, by Costis Davaras. Noyes
    Press, 1976. (ISBN 0-8155-5044-8)
        Alphabetically arranged in an encyclopedia format,
this gives all sorts of mythological, sociological and historical data concerning Crete and particulary the Minoan civilization, although other Cretans are discussed. Well illustrated
with maps, plans and photographs, this is a major contribution.

Princeton Encyclopedia of Classical Sites, edited by Richard
    Stillwell. Princeton Univ. Press, 1976. (ISBN 0-691-
    03542-3)
        Expensive but beautiful and authoritative. If you have
many questions concerning classical archeology, this will be
invaluable. Three hundred and seventy experts have written
on their own specialties and almost 3000 Greco-Roman sites
are described and often pictured. There are good maps and
a glossary.

ARMED FORCES*
see also
AIRCRAFT*

AIR POWER - HISTORY

A History of Air Power, by Basil Collier. Macmillan, 1975,
    (ISBN 0-02-52717)
        This is a basic history of the use of airpower from
the earliest days, beginning with the use of balloons in the

French Revolution, down to the Six Days War between Israel
and Egypt. It provides a realistic assessment of the actual
uses that can and cannot be made of an air arm.

ARMED FORCES - GUIDES TO THE MILITARY LIFE

The Naval Officer's Uniform Guide, by Lt. Commander J. B.
    Castano. Naval Institute Press, 1975.
        This complete handbook to the uniforms of both the
male and female officers in the United States Navy covers
every aspect of the uniform from the placement of honors,
insignia and ribbons, to the wearing of the sword. It describes every authorized U. S. Naval uniform and accessory
and gives instructions on the care and maintenance of the
uniforms.

ARMS AND ARMOR*

The Armour of Imperial Rome, by H. Russell Robinson.
    Scribner's, 1974. (ISBN 0-684-13956-1)
        Possibly one of the most beautiful books on armor
currently in print, this is an excellent source of information
concerning the various parts of the armor used in ancient
Rome. There are more than 100 line drawings and 500
plates; combined with an excellent text they make this the
definitive work on the subject.

ASTROLOGY*

Dictionary of Astrology, by H. E. Wedeck. Citadel Press,
    1973. (ISBN 0-8065-0371-8)
        The books listed in Where to Find What were excel-
lent for the interpretation of horoscopes and meanings of
various conjunctions of stars but this book attacks the situation from a different direction. It presents a definition of
about 1,250 terms and subjects as well as proper names
used in connection with astrology or astrological history.

ASTRONOMY*

Amateur Astronomer's Handbook, by James Muirden. Rev.
ed. Crowell, 1974. (ISBN 0-690-00505-9)
 The title describes the purpose of the book. Intended
for the amateur or beginning astronomer, it gives basic information on how to build an amateur observatory, how to
select and use basic telescopes and even how to build a telescope. Although written for the beginner, it can be of great
help to the serious student. In addition to discussions of
the movements of the celestial bodies and the best ways to
view them, a good glossary and bibliography as well as a
listing of future predicted eclipses of the sun and moon are
included.

Astronomy: A Handbook, ed. by G. D. Roth. Springer-
Verlag, 1975. (ISBN 0-387-06503-2)
 This is translated from a German publication and in
things scientific this is usually recommendation enough.
This one is a handbook designed to answer the questions of
amateur or professional astronomers in the fields of preci-
sion mechanics, optics and stellar photography, as well as
the more common questions concerning the study of the stars.
Particularly interesting is a chapter on mathematics applied
to astronomy intended for the amateur. There is also an
excellent bibliography.

Whitney's Star Finder: A Field Guide to the Heavens, by
Charles A. Whitney. Knopf, 1974. (ISBN 0-394-70688-
9)
 Not an intellectual approach to the subject but a field
guide to the stars which will be very helpful to anyone trying
to understand what he or she is seeing above. It has an excellent star finder and good instructions as to the best methods
of observing with the naked eye the stars, sunspots, planets,
etc.

AUTHORS*

Black American Writers, 1773-1949: A Bibliography and
Union List, ed. by Geraldine O. Matthews et al. Hall,
1975. (ISBN 0-8161-1164-2)
 A very good bibliography of the contributions of Blacks

to the field of American literature. It should be an excellent help to any institution either giving or planning to give Afro-American Studies Programs.

AUTOGRAPHS*

Autographs: A Collector's Guide, by Jerry E. Patterson.
  Crown, 1973.
      A very good guide to the ways and means of col-
lecting autographs and the various areas into which the
hobby is divided. Each type of autograph collected is discussed in a separate chapter--e.g., authors, politicians,
religious leaders--and for each type there is a description
of the material available and what the cost of acquiring it
would be. Particularly interesting are the appendices which
list, among other things, dealers and auction houses. A
bibliography of other material in the field and an excellent
index are also included.

AUTOMOBILES*

Complete Guide for Easy Car Care, by W. E. English and
  D. A. Lien. Prentice-Hall, 1975. (ISBN 0-13-160226-8)
      The basic concept of this book is the author's belief
that one-third of the money that a car owner spends on his
automobile is wasted because of lack of knowledge, which
allows unscrupulous repair men to do either incorrect or un-
necessary work. This book is aimed at teaching the automobile owner the facts of basic preventive maintenance as
well as ways to avoid becoming a victim of cheating mechanics. A variety of check lists is suggested. (Generally,
this book will prepare the car owner to face with more com-
posure the menace which is his automobile.

What Every Woman Should Know about Her Car, by Dorothy
  Jackson. Chilton, 1974. (ISBN 0-8019-6000-2)
      Although Where to Find What has several books on
the care and keeping of automobiles, I could not resist adding this one. Although it is aimed primarily at a female
audience, it will be of use to anyone, male or female. It
gives ideas for simple automobile maintenance, information
on buying new and used cars, selecting insurance coverage,

and even some hints on safe driving. The title is a little unfortunate; the book would be a good introduction for any new driver.

AVIATION

A Dictionary of Aviation, by David W. Wragg. Frederick
    Fell, 1974. (ISBN 0-8119-0236-6)
       The A to Z of the aviation industry and aviation his-
tory. It identified the major planes, famous flyers and important airlines of the world. It is alphabetically arranged
and has no illustrations but for finding little known names
or events in aviation history, it is an important tool in any
reference collection.

Who's Who in Aviation. Pergamon Press, 1974. (ISBN 0-
    08-018205-4)
       This one has been announced as being a biennial pub-
lication but no new edition has appeared as yet. It is an
excellent source of information about any of the important
names in the field of aviation whether they be developers,
engineers, pilots or airline executives. If kept up to date
this will be an excellent source book in a field previously
slighted.

BABY SITTING

Manual for Baby Sitters, by Marion S. Lowndes. Rev. ed.
    Little, Brown, 1961. (ISBN 0-316-53397-1)
       This is a guide to help teenagers take care of the
young children entrusted to their care. It emphasizes their
responsibilities and gives hints on meeting minor crises.

BALLET*

A Dictionary of Ballet, by G. L. B. Wilson. 3rd ed.
    Theatre Arts, 1974. (ISBN 0-87830-039-2)
       The books listed in Where to Find What concentrated

on giving the stories or plots of the various ballets. This volume gives definitions of terms used in the field and fully discusses the way that they are used. Its major limitation is that it ignores Russian ballet almost entirely, but it is excellent for terms used in English, German and American ballet.

BANKRUPTCY

The best source of information concerning the Bankruptcy Laws of an individual state would naturally be the Code of Laws generally published by the state legislature. The very good small book listed here summarizes the laws for the whole country clearly and well. Anyone considering legal action should consult an attorney but this book outlines the debtor's and creditor's rights and obligations. It summarizes the various rules and regulations for the whole country.

Bankruptcy, by the Editors of Gould Press. Gould Press, 1976. (ISBN 0-87526-193-0)

BARTENDING

Trader Vic's Bartender's Guide, ed. by Shirley Sarvis. Revised and expanded edition. Doubleday, 1972. (ISBN 0-384-06805-0)
Not being a drinking man, it did not occur to me to include this book in the Where to Find What, but repeated requests persuaded me to investigate the books available and there seems to be general agreement that this is one of the very best books on the subject. It has directions for more than 1000 different drinks. It was intended as a guide for professional bartenders but the directions are clear enough that even the neophyte can mix a passable drink immediately or a good one with practice.

BATTLES *

Sea Battles: A Reference Guide, by Michael Sanderson.

David and Charles, 1975.
  This is an alphabetically arranged listing of all the
battles from the battle of Lade in 494 B.C. to the battle of
Leyte Gulf in 1944.   Each of more than 250 battles is concisely described and many are accompanied by diagrams and
maps of the battle actions.   The alphabetical listing is complemented by a supplement which arranges each action chronologically.

BATTLESHIPS
see
SHIPS

BEES AND BEEKEEPING

Amateur Beekeeping, by Edward L. Sechrist.   Devin-Adair,
  1955.   (ISBN 0-8159-5001-2)
  Although getting quite old this book is still one of the
very best for the amateur beekeeper and can be easily understood by anyone with an interest in the subject.

The Bee Keeper's Encyclopedia, by Alexander S. Deans.
  Gale, 1975.   (Reprint of 1949 ed.)   (ISBN 0-8103-4176-X)
  This is the book on beekeeping for both the beginner
and the expert.   It has been respected now for thirty years.

Bees and Beekeeping, by Roger A. Morse.   Cornell University Press, 1975.   (ISBN 0-8014-0884-9)

The Complete Guide to Beekeeping, by Roger A. Morse.   Rev.
  ed.   Dutton, 1974.   (ISBN 0-87690-126-7)
  Intended for the serious keeper of bees, these two
books nevertheless are excellent beginning source books for
information not only on types of bees but the best ways to
treat them and to profit from them.

BIBLE*

Oxford Bible Atlas, ed. by Herbert G. May and G. H. Hunt.   2nd
  ed.   Oxford University Press, 1974.   (ISBN 0-19-211556-1)

Although Where to Find What had many Biblical references, it did not include a Bible Atlas, so the reissue of an outstanding work in the field is welcome. This book is divided into four parts. The first is a historical description of the countries of the Near East, the second consists of full color maps with descriptive text which describes the topography, climate and archeological finds. The third section is devoted to archeology of the Biblical area, and finally there is a gazetteer which not only locates places but tells something about each place. The book is well illustrated with photographs as well as maps.

BIBLIOGRAPHY

Although there has been some criticism of Where to Find What because of its failure to list bibliographies, it is my belief that a book of this nature, intended for ready reference in the small or medium-sized library, does not warrant the inclusion of general bibliographies. Bibliographies are included under specific subject headings where applicable, but basically I feel that most bibliographies fall outside the intended scope of this publication.

BIOGRAPHY*

Recognizing the growing need to reduce the search time needed to locate biographical information, both Marquis and the Gale Research Company have recently published master indices to a wide range of biographic references.

Biographical Dictionaries, Master Index, ed. by Dennis Le Beau and Gary C. Turbett. First Edition, 3 Volumes, 1975-76. Gale Research, 1976. (ISBN 0-8103-1077-5)
This is by far the superior set of the two new publications. It indexes more than 725,000 entries from 53 biographical dictionaries as well as other works of collective biography. The books selected for inclusion in this set are primarily American in orientation but all biographees are indexed, whether American or foreign. It is anticipated that revision will be biennial but it is unclear whether a full-scale revision of the whole work is contemplated, or merely supplements adding the most recent publications.

Index to All Books, 1974. ed. by Editorial Staff of Marquis
    Who's Who Publications. Marquis, 1974. (ISBN 0-8379-
    1401-6)
    This is a combined index to all Marquis publications
and an excellent time-saving device. It is, however, limited
to the 200,000 biographies which have appeared in the various
Marquis Who's Whos. If the Gale publication had not recently
appeared I would be very excited over this item.

BIRDS *

The Dell Encyclopedia of Birds, by Bertel Bruun. Delacorte,
    1974. (ISBN 0-440-01785-8)
    A field guide intended for the novice or beginning bird
watcher. It is pocket-sized, which makes it excellent for
the bird watcher but not so good for the library.

Encyclopedia of Cage and Aviary Birds, by Cyril H. Rogers.
    Macmillan, 1975.
    This is a comprehensive treatment of the subject of
caged birds, equally useful for the beginning breeder of birds
or for more advanced students. It has detailed descriptions,
often accompanied by excellent color photographs, of almost
all cage birds in the United States. For each it gives information on the type of cage needed, feeding, and the best
times and ways of breeding. In addition, there is a section
dealing with diseases which may attack cage birds. Written
simply, it can be easily understood by everyone.

World Atlas of Birds, edited by Peter Scott. Random House,
    1974. (ISBN 0-394-49483-0)
    This is an expensive and beautiful book which might
be more at home on the coffee table than on the library
shelves, but it is good for describing the ecological and environmental locations of various bird species. It is not particularly good for bird identification but is excellent for the
various habitats of birds around the world and for notes on
each of the world's bird families. The book is illustrated
by color paintings and the text is excellent.

BIRTH CERTIFICATES

Where to Write for Birth and Death Records. U.S. Public

Health Service. Government Printing Office. Revised
as necessary.
    A listing of sources to which one can write to get
information concerning vital statistics and to obtain birth or
death certificates.

BLACKS*
see also
AUTHORS; FOLKLORE;
NAMES, PERSONAL;
CIVIL RIGHTS

The Ebony Handbook, edited by The Editors of Ebony Maga-
    zine. Johnson Publishing Company, Chicago, 1974.
    (ISBN 0-87485-064-9)
    This is a worthy successor to the Negro Handbook
published in 1966 and continues the excellent coverage of the
original book with additional subjects and enlargement of
many others. It is a good source for statistical information
as well as documented articles. It is possibly the best
single reference source on the black experience and is highly
recommended for every library.

Who's Who among Black Americans, Vol. I: 1975-76. Who's
    Who Among Black Americans, 3202 Doolittle Drive,
    Northbrook, Illinois, 60062. 1976. (ISBN 0-915130-05-X)
    This provides information on 10, 000 black notables cur-
rently important in all fields of endeavor. There is some
overlap with other Who's Who-type materials but for the most
part these are new biographies. There are indexes to careers
and to geographic locations.

Chronological History of the Negro in America, by Peter M.
    Bergman and Mort N. Bergman. Harper & Row, 1969.
    (ISBN 0-06-010303-5)
    A chronology of the black experience in America with
short notations about historical events and cultural developments. There is a good index and bibliography. A good
book for any library needing information on black history
and culture.

BOATS AND BOATING*

<u>Sailing Boats of the World: A Guide by Classes</u>, edited by
Rhonda Budd. Prentice-Hall, 1974. (ISBN 0-13-786129-
X)
     This is about the most definitive book published on
the many types of boats operating in American waters. It
includes over 1, 800 different classes of sailboats from the
largest down to the sailing surf boards. If it is classed as
a boat, it will be listed in this reference. For each type
of boat listed there is given the name of the designer, the
first year it was made, the country of origin, and specifications and plans for building the boat. There is a listing of
boat manufacturers and equipment suppliers along with their
addresses.

BOOK PRICES*

<u>Book Collector's Handbook of Values, 1976-1977</u>. 2nd ed.,
by Van Allen Bradley. G. P. Putnam & Sons, 1975.
(ISBN 0-399-11482-3)
     The author of <u>Gold in Your Attic</u> has come up with
another excellent guide to the value of fine books, first editions and general collectibles. The book is alphabetically
arranged by author (or by title if no author is given) and
gives the values of books in good condition. If the book has
a weakness, it is that it deals primarily with American and
British publications of the 19th and 20th centuries, but within
these limitations it is an excellent book not only for the book
dealer or the collector but also for the librarian who has to
answer patrons' questions concerning the possible value of
books in their possession.

BOOK REVIEWS*

<u>Current Book Review Citations</u>. H. W. Wilson, 1976.
(Annual)
     This addition to the excellent series of Wilson indexes
should be of great benefit to all persons needing book review
information. It is an accumulation of all book review citations

found in the other Wilson indexes, thus covering more than
1000 periodicals in all fields.   This means it will locate
many technical and ephemeral book reviews not previously
listed.   In time, it may well be the premier publication of
this kind.

BOOKS - BANNED

Banned Books, by Anne L. Haight.   3rd ed.   Bowker, 1970.
   (ISBN 0-8352-0204-6)
     This is a thoroughly indexed listing of all the major
books that have been banned, for whatever reason.   It gives
the normal bibliographic information including author, date
of publication, etc. , and then indicates why, where, when
and by whom the book was banned.   Excellent for listing of
court decisions and censorship.   There is a good bibliography.

BOOKS - PLOTS AND CHARACTERS*
see also
SHAKESPEARE

Dictionary of Fictional Characters, by Fred Urquhart.   Rev.
    ed.   Writer, 1974.   (ISBN 0-87116-085-4)
     This book identifies over 20, 000 characters in works
of fiction, including poems, plays, novels, short stores and
operas.   It is better for early English and American works
than for modern writers but is an essential publication for almost any library.   There are three parts to the book.   Part
I is alphabetically arranged by characters' name, with a discussion of each character in relation to the work in which he
or she appears.   It also cites author and date of the work.
Parts II and III are author and title indices, which are not
particularly valuable given the reason most persons will be
using this work.

Who's Who in Children's Books: A Treasury of the Familiar
    Characters of Childhood, by Margery Fisher.   Holt,
    Rinehart and Winston, 1975.   (ISBN 0-03-015091-4)
     An alphabetical arrangement of the characters of
children's fiction, with names listed as they appear in the

books. In other words, Little Lord Fauntleroy is under L, and so on. It is a delight to read and even to browse in since it has many illustrations, some in color. The author says it is not primarily a reference book but as well as being enjoyable, it will help greatly in identifications temporarily forgotten.

Then there is a book dealing with fantasy and science fiction which will be of interest to all its fans:

An Atlas of Fantasy, by J. B. Post. Mirage Press, 1973. (ISBN 0-88358-108-6)
If you ever wondered about the exact location of Oz, Treasure Island, or Narnia, this is the book to answer your questions. It is not complete since many imaginary places are not mapped, but for those that are, the maps are clearly reproduced with a commentary by the author.

BOXING*

Encyclopedia of World Boxing Champions Since 1882, by John D. McCallum. Chilton, 1975. (ISBN 0-8019-6161-7)
This is a biographical dictionary of all the men who have held boxing championships from the time of John L. Sullivan to the present day. For most there are pictures as well as mini-biographies giving a brief outline of the life and career of each boxer. This is a particularly valuable book because all weight classes from flyweight to heavyweight are included. It is fairly easy to find information elsewhere on the heavier ranks but can be more difficult for the smaller boxers.

BRAND NAMES

Thomas's Register of American Manufacturers. Thomas Publications. Annual since 1905.
This multi-volume annual publication is divided into four parts. Part one is an alphabetical listing of product classifications. For each type of manufactured article there is a geographical listing showing where it is made; for

example, under caskets there is a full listing by states and cities of all casket manufacturers in the United States. Part two is an alphabetical listing of manufacturers, showing what each company manufactures. Part three is a product and trademark and brand name index; for example, if you want to know who manufactures Brand-X, look under that name and it will tell you who the manufacturer is. Part four is a collection of catalogs of manufacturers, arranged in alphabetical order.

Trade News Dictionary, ed. by Ellen T. Crowley. First edition. 2 vols. Gale Research, 1976. (ISBN 0-8103-0692-1)
   A guide to trade names, brand names, coined names, model names, product names and design names, with addresses of their manufacturers, importers, marketers or distributors.

BUDGET, PERSONAL
see
PERSONAL FINANCE

BUTTERFLIES

Butterflies of the World, by H. L. Lewis. Follett, 1973. (ISBN 0-695-81434-0)
   This is a beautiful but expensive book with photographs of more than 5000 different butterflies in full color. One interesting aspect of the photos is that usually both the upper and lower sides of the butterfly are shown, making for a more positive identification. Although the textual matter is very brief, it is adequate in connection with the illustrations, and between the two it is possible to identify practically any butterfly in the world. The value of the book is enhanced by keys to the life sizes of the butterflies pictured as well as general identification notes. It not only is the most complete book on the subject available but easily the most beautiful.

A Field Guide to the Butterflies of North America East of the Great Plains, by Alexander B. Klots. Houghton Mifflin, 1951. (ISBN 0-395-07865-2)

This volume in the Peterson Field Guide Series, like the others, is an excellent pocket-sized book intended for use in the field. It uses a system of comparative markings, patterns and distinctions to make identification easy. Although neither as comprehensive nor as beautiful as the Lewis book mentioned above, it probably is more suitable for the average collector of butterflies since its size makes it easier to handle. While many of the pictures are not in color, all are of the type likely to be helpful to the beginner as well as the seasoned collector.

CALCULATORS

The Calculator Handbook, by A. N. Feldzamen and Faye Henle. Berkley Publishing Corp., 1973. (ISBN 0-425-02440-7)

Few items have found so much immediate acceptance as the pocket calculator. It is used in the home, for shopping, or figuring income tax, and in countless other ways. This book is intended to supply information on how to select the proper calculator for your needs, how to use it once purchased, and general guidelines on getting the most use from a calculator.

CALORIES
see
FOOD

CENSORSHIP
see
BOOKS - BANNED

CERAMICS

Dictionary of Ceramics, by A. E. Dodd. Littlefield-Adams, 1964. (ISBN 0-8226-0173-7)

This is an excellent source for information on physical

and chemical data as well as definitions of terms used in pottery, glass, enamels, cement and concrete and other ceramic materials.

CHARACTERS IN LITERATURE
see
BOOKS - PLOTS AND CHARACTERS

CHRONOLOGY*

Timetables of History, by Bernard Grun. Simon & Schuster, 1975. (ISBN 0-671-21682-1)
   Those of you who are old enough will remember a similar book entitled Who Was When. That book presented historical information in tabular form, with various categories of people arranged in columns so that one could locate, say, Beethoven and find who the important artists, writers and politicians of his era were. This book does much the same thing, with the addition of historical events as well. There is an excellent index and the book will be of help to students who want to relate men and women to events or to other fields of endeavor.

CITIES*

Contemporary Metropolitan America, ed. by John S. Adams. 4 vols. Ballinger Publishing Co., 1976. (ISBN 0-88410-425-7)
   This four-volume set encompasses the human and economic development of America's 20 largest metropolitan areas. It was a project of American Geographers Comparative Metropolitan Analysis Project and has been written by a body of eminent scholars. Vol. 1, Cities in the Nations Historical Metropolitan Area; Vol. 2, 19th Century Ports; Vol. 3, 19th Century Inland Centers and Ports; Vol. 4, 20th Century Cities. The four books together provide both a historical and sociological approach to present-day America, but each volume may be purchased separately.

Comparative Atlas of America's Great Cities: Twenty Metro-
    politan Regions, ed. by Ronald Abler.   Univ. of Minne-
    sota Pr., 1976.   (ISBN 0-8166-0767-2)
        Although published by a different publisher this is also
a project of the American Geographers Comparative Metropolitan Analysis Project.   It has over 1000 maps with full textual explanation of the 20 most populous metropolitan areas.
It covers such problems as the current developing pattern of
urban growth in the areas, the problems that growth entails
and general statistics concerning urban life today.   A good
glossary, an index, a gazetteer and a location guide are included.

CITIZEN'S BAND RADIO

        Seldom has a fad, hobby or avocation hit the American
scene with such impact as the CB radio.   Songs have been
written about it, people have praised it and condemned it,
but it is a fact of life and one about which libraries are re-
ceiving an increasing number of questions.
        The proper operation of the citizen's band radio and
the regulations concerning it are a responsibility of the Federal Communications Commission and as such appear in the
following government publications.

Code of Federal Regulations.   Title 47 - Telecommunications.
    Part 15.   Government Printing Office.   Revised annually.
    (GS4. 108:1, 47/)

        Prior to appearance in the Code, all Federal Regula-
tions appear in:

The Federal Register.   Government Printing Office.   Daily.
    (GS 4: 107)

The Complete FM Two-Way Radio Handbook, by Clayton L.
    Hallmark.   TAB Books, 1974.   (ISBN 0-8306-4735-X)
        The book starts with a general survey of two-way
radio and progresses from there to a discussion of the FM
fundamentals as applied to citizen's band and other two-way
radios.   An appendix gives the full text of the FCC rules
as they apply to CB radio, and there is a listing of recommended repair equipment.

Practical C.B. Radio Troubleshooting and Repair, by David
F. Norman. TAB Books, 1975. (ISBN 0-8306-5754-1)

Official C.B. Operator's Kit, by the Editors of Consumer
Guide. Consumer Guide, 1975.
This kit includes a manual and log and the necessary
information needed to master the language used, the techniques and the rules. It has a CB road map and a code card
included.

CITY PLANNING

The Municipal Yearbook. Washington, D.C.: International
City Management Association. Annual since 1934.
This is the single best source for answering questions
concerning municipal governments and cities. It is an annual
compilation of articles and statistical data dealing with all
phases of city management and government. It covers current trends, issues and activities, municipal finance, man-
power and public safety. In addition, it has many statistical
charts showing latest information on salaries paid, depart-
mental budgets, etc. Each annual issue carries the latest
information in the field of city planning.

CIVIL RIGHTS*

Civil Rights: A Current Guide to the People, Organizations
and Events, edited by Joan M. Burke. 2nd ed. Bowker,
1974. (ISBN 0-8352-0722-6)
This is the second edition of a book listed in Where
to Find What. It is intended primarily as a guide for news-
men but is an excellent source of information for the general
user. It is excellent for biographical identification and organizations. A must for any library which receives civil
rights questions.

CIVIL SERVICE

The announcements of the Federal Civil Service are

available at your local post office. They give all pertinent data concerning how to apply, location of the position, education and/or experience required, and salary.

The Arco Publishing Company has an entire series of Civil Service Test Tutors which covers practically every form of Civil Service employment.

The following are study outlines for general preparation for Civil Service Tests. In addition there are 155 individual job titles for which study guides are available. For these, see the Arco Publishing Company catalog. Since all the following are from Arco, only the titles, dates and ISBN numbers are given.

Civil Service Handbook. 4th ed. 1965. (ISBN 0-668-00040-6)

Federal Service Entrance Examinations. 9th ed. 1974. (ISBN 0-668-00528-9)

General Entrance Series. 1969. (ISBN 0-668-01861-1)

General Test Practice for 92 U.S. Jobs. 6th ed. 1971. (ISBN 0-668-00011-2)

Homestudy Course for Civil Service Jobs. 4th ed. 1972. (ISBN 0-668-01587-X)

Federal Career Directory, A Guide for G.P.O. College Students. U.S. Civil Service Commission. Annual. (CS 1. 7/4 C18/)

This directory presents specific information about Federal careers and the agencies that employ college graduates. It will enable the student to better prepare for a federal career by providing him/her with some idea of the type of positions involved as well as the necessary academic preparation.

CLERGYMEN
see also
INCOME TAX

Who's Who in Religion, 1975-76. Marquis Who's Who, 1975. (ISBN 0-8379-1601-1)

This is a standard Who's Who of clergymen serving

in the United States, giving all the usual data associated with that series.

CLOCKS AND WATCHES*

Where to Find What had a listing of books dealing with the history of clocks and watches and the people who make them. The following book is intended for the person who wants to repair watches as a hobby. It is intended for the beginner and assumes no previous knowledge of watch- or clock-making. It describes in easily understood terms how they work and the various types of movements found, as well as the things that can go wrong with each type of clock or watch. There are precise directions for dismantling, correcting and reassembling various makes, accompanied by clear drawings. The user of this book will usually not have any pieces left over after completing the watch repairs.

Handbook of Watch and Clock Repairs, by H. G. Harris.
    Rev. ed. Emerson Books, 1972. (ISBN 0-87523-141-1)

A related book, intended for the advanced amateur, is the following:

Advanced Watch and Clock Repairs, by H. G. Harris. Emerson Books, 1973. (ISBN 0-87523-181-0)

COLLEGES AND UNIVERSITIES*

Dictionary of College Transfer Information, prepared by
    American Schools Association. Simon & Schuster, 1974.
    (ISBN 0-671-187104-4)
       In an age in which more than half of the students entering college drop out or transfer to another school before graduation, this is an important publication. The main section of the book consists of an alphabetically arranged list of colleges giving the usual information concerning degrees offered, curricular and extra-curricular activities and a section on the information needed for transfer: e.g., minimum grades accepted, deadline for application, maximum hours which may be transferred, and possibilities of financial aid.

COMMERCIAL PRODUCTS

Thomas's Register of American Manufacturers.   Thomas
   Publications.   Annual since 1905.
      This multi-volume annual publication is divided into
four parts.   Part one is an alphabetical listing of product
classification.   For each type of manufactured article there
is a geographical listing showing where it is made; for example, under caskets there is a full listing by states and
cities of all casket manufacturers in the United States.   Part
two is an alphabetical listing of manufacturers, showing what
each company manufactures.   Part three is a product and
trademark and brand name index; for example, if you want to
know who manufactures Brand-X, look under that name and
it will tell you who the manufacturer is.   Part four is a
collection of catalogs of manufacturers, arranged in alphabetical order.

COMPOSERS *

Index to Biographies of Contemporary Composers, by Storm
   Bull.   2 vols.   Scarecrow Press, 1964-1974.   Vol. 1
   (ISBN 0-8108-0065-9); Vol. 2 (ISBN 0-8108-9734-3)
      I did not include volume one of this work in the origi-
nal book since it was becoming dated, but the appearance of
volume two updates and complements the other to such an
extent that any library dealing with questions about composers
should have both.   Together they provide an alphabetical index to almost 200 biographical sources.

Biographical Directory of American Music, by Charles Eu-
   gene Claghorn.   Parker, 1973.   (ISBN 0-13-076331-4)
      Very short descriptive biographical sketches of many
little known American composers.   The book is more comprehensive than most such directories in its coverage, but
also more scanty in the information provided.

COMPUTERS

Computer Acronyms Handbook, by Donald D. Spencer.
   Prentice-Hall, 1974.   (ISBN 0-13-164863-2)

Few things in life are as confusing as computers and one of the most confusing aspects is the many acronyms which are used in speaking or writing about them. This book, while not strictly following the definition of acronyms, is an excellent source of information for persons trying to find the meanings of various abbreviations, acronyms and words in this field.

Computer Dictionary, by Charles J. Sippl and Charles P. Sippl. 2nd ed. Howard J. Sams, 1974. (ISBN 0-672-20943-8)

While acronyms are always confusing, many words in the computer field are equally so. There are many computer dictionaries but the members of our Electrical Engineering Department tell me that this is the best source of definitions of words and terms dealing with computers and computer applications.

The Way Things Work Book of the Computer: an Illustrated Encyclopedia of Information Science, Cybernetics and Data Processing. Simon and Schuster, 1974. (ISBN 0-671-21900-6)

As an uninformed and thoroughly intimidated reader, I found this book to be a little technical, but it is an excellent introduction that contains much information presented in a fairly easily understood way. The illustrations are excellent. This should be valuable for the non-technical library.

CONSUMER INFORMATION

Capital Contacts in Consumerism. Fraser/Ruder & Finn. 1976.

This is a Who's Who directory to consumer contacts, listing programs, services, addresses and phone numbers of the people in Federal agencies, State consumer agencies, national consumer groups and many other sources of information. It is currently the most comprehensive and up-to-date source on consumer information personnel.

Consumer Information Handbook: Europe and North America, by Hans B. Thorelli and Sarah V. Thorelli. Praeger, 1974. (ISBN 0-275-28770-X)

A directory to consumer information systems in Europe and North America, this tells how they operate and their influence on manufacturers and sellers alike. This is the first of three planned volumes dealing with consumer organizations.

Consumer's Handbook, ed. by Paul Fargis. Revised and
    updated. Hawthorn Books, 1974. (ISBN 0-8015-51746-X)
    A compilation of facts concerning finances, food, housing, equipment, etc. collected from a variety of sources. While all the information is available from government publications, this presents them in a ready reference format which makes the book a worthwhile addition to a reference collection.

Consumer's Sourcebook: A Directory and Guide to Govern-
    ment Organizations, Associations, Centers and Institutes,
    Media Service Company and Trademark Information and
    Biographical Materials Leading to Consumer Topics,
    Sources of Recourse and Advisory Information, ed. by
    Paul Wasserman and Jean Morgan. Gale Research, 1974.
    (ISBN 0-8103-0381-7)
    With a subtitle like that one, there is little need for an annotation. This is an excellent source book for such information as telephone numbers and addresses as well as the names of important personnel to contact when lodging complaints or requesting information. Also a good source of information on trade names and trademarks.

Guide to Federal Consumer Services, ed. by U. S. Office of
    Consumer Affairs. Government Printing Office, 1971.
    (PrEx 16. 8: Se 6)
    This directory lists in one place the vast number of persons, services and programs offered by the government to aid the consumer. It is arranged by agency and for each it tells what its program is, how it is enforced and how to apply for information. There is a dictionary of agency initials and acronyms.

State Administrative Officials Classified by Functions.
    Council of State Governments, 1975. (ISBN 0-87292-
    013-5)
    This is a supplement to The Book of the States, mentioned in Where to Find What. Under the heading "Consumer Protection" you will find the state agency dealing with Consumer Information.

CORPORATIONS

The types of questions about corporations will vary from library to library, but the following books should be available in all but the smallest libraries.

Moody's Manuals, published by Moody's Investor's Service, Inc. Annual.
    Although intended primarily for investors, these manuals are an excellent source of information on almost every business within the United States. For each company, there is given the history, the management (both managers and directors), an analysis of the things manufactured or produced, and a consolidated income statement and balance sheet. This is the ultimate source of information about American companies. The Moody manuals are in five sections: 1. Bank and Finance; 2. Industrials; 3. Public Utilities; 4. Transportation; 5. Municipals.

Standard and Poor's Register of Corporations, Directors and Executives. Standard and Poor's. Annual. First published 1928.
    This is primarily a directory to officers and directors of corporations, but it is also much more than that. It has an opening section that gives and explains the Standard Industrial Classification (SIC) Index as well as a corporate listing giving addresses, telephone numbers, zip codes, etc.

Thomas's Register of American Manufacturers. Thomas Publications. Annual since 1905.
    This multi-volume annual publication is divided into four parts. Part one is an alphabetical listing of product classifications. For each type of manufactured article there is a geographical listing showing where it is made; for example, under caskets there is a full listing by states and cities of all casket manufacturers in the United States. Part two is an alphabetical listing of manufacturers, showing what each company manufactures. Part three is a product and trademark and brand name index; for example, if you want to know who manufactures Brand-X, look under that name and it will tell you who the manufacturer is. Part four is a collection of catalogs of manufacturers, arranged in alphabetical order.

CORRESPONDENCE COURSES

There are two inexpensive publications which are valuable in locating extension and correspondence courses with regional accreditation. They are:

For extension courses offered by universities and colleges:

Guide to Independent Study through Correspondence Instruction. National University Extension Association. Washington, D. C. Published biennially.

Correspondence courses offered by private schools.

Private Home Study in the United States. National Home Study Council. Washington, D. C. Published biennially.

COUNTRY AND WESTERN MUSIC
see
MUSIC - COUNTRY AND WESTERN

COURTS MARTIAL

Libraries will probably receive relatively few questions about the reasons for and the methods involved in courts martial, but should such a question arise, there is no better publication to answer it than a loose-leaf publication of the Department of Defense:

A Manual of Courts Martial. U. S. Department of Defense. Government Printing Office. Revised ed., 1969. (D1. 15)

For definitions used in military law:

Military Law Dictionary, ed. by Richard C. Dahl and J. F. Whelan. Oceana. 1960. (ISBN 0-379-00042-3)

CROSSWORD PUZZLES*

My earlier book listed books on how to make puzzles and a dictionary of words intended for the solution of puzzles. The following title attacks the subject from a different angle, giving a history of the fascination with crosswords as well as some hints on solving difficult puzzles.

Crossword Puzzles: Their History and Their Cult, by Roger
    Millington. Thomas Nelson, 1975. (ISBN 0-847-6471-5)

Funk and Wagnall's Crossword Puzzle Word Finder, by Ed-
    mund L. Schwartz and Leon F. Landovitz. Crowell,
    1974. (ISBN 0-308-10126-X)
This is not really a crossword puzzle dictionary but it will give great help in solving even the most difficult puzzles. It is based on the assumption that you will have at least two letters of any desired word and is therefore arranged by the number of letters in the word and then by the two letters you know. These letters are arranged by any number of possible combinations so that the desired ones can be located. Since it does not give definitions but rather lists of words, it really is not quite fair to use it in solving puzzles, but for those who want answers at any price it will be a great help.

DAMS

Water Encyclopedia, ed. by David Keith Todd. Water In-
    formation Center. 1970. (ISBN 0-912394-01-3)
This is a practical reference volume containing a variety of water resources data, facts and statistics. It is divided into mini-chapters: climate and precipitation, hydrologic elements, surface water, ground water, water use, waste and pollution control, water quality, water resources management, agencies and organizations and constants and conversion factors. Each chapter is a wealth of statistical information in tabular form; "Table 7-2: Major Dams in the United States" lists all the dams in the country over 250 feet high and covering more than a million cubic yards. For each one is given the location, the river dammed, the length, the height and its purpose as well as date of construction. Table 7-4 lists the major dams of the world.

DEPRECIATION

There is a very good discussion and a chart on the potential depreciation of automobiles in the following book:

Sylvia Porter's Money Book, by Sylvia Porter. Doubleday, 1975. (ISBN 0-385-08484-6)
The subtitle of this book is "How to earn it, spend it, save it, invest it, borrow it and use it to better your life." Written by an outstanding newspaper writer on personal finance, this book is as good a discussion of home budgets and budgetary problems as I have seen. It covers almost any conceivable fiscal problem likely to face a family and discusses it in easily understood language. I could think of no better wedding present for any couple.

Depreciation Guide 1975. Commerce Clearing House, 1975.
This is a simplified and easily understood discussion of the ways to compute depreciation. It is well supplied with tables, lists and examples which help with clarification. It is published by the leading publisher of tax materials.

For tables showing depreciation schedules see:

The Thorndike Encyclopedia of Banking and Financial Tables, by David Thorndike. Warren, Gorham & Lamont, Inc. 1974. (ISBN 0-88262-062-2)
This book contains tables for real estate, depreciation, compound interest, annuity interest, savings, installment loans, rebates, mortgage values and stock yields. There are tables to show every possible combination of percentages and years to be calculated. This book will answer quickly most of your financial statistical questions.

DINOSAURS

The Dinosaur Book, by Edwin H. Colbert. McGraw-Hill, 1951. (ISBN 0-07-011665-2)
Although written for the teenage audience, this is a highly reliable book which can be used with any age group. It was prepared for the American Museum of Natural History and is well indexed. Good textual material combined with excellent illustrations make this a valuable book.

DRAMATISTS

Contemporary Dramatists, edited by James Vinson. St.
    Martin's Press. 1973.
      This massive book lists practically every living dram-
atist writing in English. Each person has been asked to
submit a biography, a bibliography of all published works
giving the dates of publication and, in the case of American
works, the date of first performance. Any theater-related
activities of the dramatist are also listed. In addition to
the comments of the dramatists themselves, each one is
discussed in a critical essay by an outstanding critic of the
theater. The book can be recommended highly but it must
be remembered that these biographies are written by the
dramatists themselves and may reflect the "halo effect."

DREAMS

      The two most common types of questions concerning
dreams which will come to you as a reference librarian, are
those requiring a scientific or psychological explanation, and
those which are looking for a mysterious or magical interpretation.
      There are two serious books which should be in prac-
tically every library. Each is the work of an important
psychiatrist. While they differ greatly in interpretation, each
is important for a scientific understanding of why we dream.

Interpretation of Dreams, by Sigmund Freud, ed. by James
    J. Strachey. Basic Books, 1954. (ISBN 0-465-03411-X)

The Forgotten Language: an Introduction to the Understand-
    ing of Dreams, Fairy Tales and Myths, by Erich Fromm.
    Holt, Rinehart & Winston, 1951. (ISBN 0-03-025535-X)

      Then there are two which give a mystical or mysteri-
ous interpretation of dreams by telling what each thing
dreamed about signifies.

The Dreamer's Dictionary: The Complete Guide to Inter-
    preting Your Dreams, by Stearn Robinson and Tom
    Corbett. Taplinger, 1974. (ISBN 0-8008-2270-6)

Zolar's Everything You Want to Know About Dreams, Lucky
  Numbers, Omens, Oils and Incense, by Bruce King.
  Arc Books, 1972. (ISBN 0-668-02600-6)

DRUG ABUSE

Everything You Wanted to Know about Drug Abuse ... But
  Were Afraid to Ask, by Charles L. Winick. Marcel
  Dekker, 1974. (ISBN 0-8247-6145-6)
    This is intended for use with young people and tries
to anticipate their questions concerning this vital subject.
The main portion of the book is devoted to a series of questions and answers on all phases of the subject. It is written
by a Professor of Toxicology at Duquesne University and the
answers given, while scientific, are written in an interesting
and useful manner. In addition to the questions and answers,
there is a glossary of terms used to understand drug abuse.

Guide to Drug Information, by Winifred Sewell. Drug Intel-
  ligence Publications, 1976. (ISBN 0-914768-21-2)
    This is an excellent bibliography dealing with litera-
ture on drug information and ways to put that information to
work. This balance of bibliography and problem solving
makes this an invaluable addition.

State Administrative Officials Classified by Function. Council of State Governments, 1975. (ISBN 0-87292-013-5)
    This is a supplement to The Book of the States, men-
tioned in Where to Find What. Under the heading of "Drug
Abuse" you will find the state agencies dealing with this subject.

EARTHQUAKES

Earthquake History of the United States. 2 vols. U.S.
  Coast and Geodetic Survey. Rev. ed. Government
  Printing Office, 1961. (C4. 19/2: 41-1)
    This lists and describes the effects of the major
earthquakes that have hit the continental United States up
through the year of 1955.

ELECTRONICS

Electronics Engineers' Handbook, ed. by Donald G. Fink.
    McGraw-Hill, 1975. (ISBN 0-07-020980-X)
        This is a standard handbook approach to the field of
electronics, written from the point of view of practical application rather than theoretical discussion. It covers well
almost every conceivable phase of the subject.

Modern Dictionary of Electronics, by Rudolf F. Graf. 4th
    ed. Howard W. Sams, 1972. (ISBN 0-672-20852-0)
        A very comprehensive dictionary of electronic terms
giving definitions for almost 20,000 words and phrases. The
definitions are short but precise and easily understood. For
the more frequently mispronounced words there is a pronunciation guide.

ENERGY

The Energy Directory. Environment Information Center,
    New York, 1974. (L.C. 74-79869)
        The problem of energy and energy conservation is just
beginning to be really felt in this country and for a people
brought up on cheap and plentiful energy resources, it is a
traumatic experience. This book lists and describes almost
2000 governmental and private agencies involved in this field.
It is a valuable tool for anyone wanting to locate agencies
involved in specific research or service.

        For books and printed materials dealing with the
problem:

Buyer's Guide to Environmental Media: Energy. Environ-
    ment Information Center, New York, 1974.

        For discussions of various types of energy:

New Low Cost Sources of Energy for the Home, with a
    Complete Illustrated Catalog, by Peter Clegg. Gardon
    Way, 1975. (ISBN 0-88266-060-8)
        Although any catalog is quickly out of date, this book
should be valuable for many years to come. It discusses
many types of energy available, solar, wind, water, various

combustibles, and for each type gives some idea of how it
can be used and the relative costs involved as well as illustrated designs.

For a listing of State Agencies concerning energy:

State Administrative Officials Classified by Function. Coun-
    cil of State Governments, 1975. (ISBN 0-87292-013-5)
    This is a supplement to the Book of the States men-
tioned in Where to Find What. Under "Energy" you will find
all agencies dealing with that function.

Energy Atlas: A Who's Who to Information, ed. by Eric
    Tower. Fraser, Ruder and Finn, 1976.
    This is not only a Who's Who which identifies the
people and agencies to contact concerning energy problems;
it is also a unique cross-referenced index to energy questions. It will help you find information in the fields of con-
servation, energy management, fossil energy resources and
research development. Currently it is the most up-to-date
and comprehensive guide to energy information available.

2007648

FACTS*
see also
TRIVIA

Book of Firsts, by Patrick Robertson. Potter, 1974.
    (ISBN 0-517-51577-6)
    Any book of this kind must be compared with Famous
First Facts by Joseph Nathan Kane. While this one does not
quite measure up to the original, in some ways it is superi-
or. It brings the facts up to the year 1974 and has actually
more entries, but it is British in origin and shows its bias
at times in such ways as British spelling. If only one book
can be ordered take Kane, but if you can afford two, this
will be helpful.

How It Started, by Webb Garrison. Abingdon Press, 1972.
    (ISBN 0-687-17605-0)
    The beginnings of customs, beliefs, ideas and inven-
tions.

FELLOWSHIPS AND GRANTS*

The Foundation Center Source Book. 2 vols. The Foundation Center, ed. by Terry-Diane Beck and Alexis T.
   Gersumsky. Columbia University Press, 1975. V. 1
   (ISBN 0-87954-007-9) V. 2 (ISBN 0-87954-008-7)
   This is an expensive source book of information on
the major foundations which grant funds for fellowships and
research. It gives detailed information on the programs,
policies and application procedures for each foundation as
well as information concerning its fiscal situation and a listing of recent grants. This is probably the most comprehensive compilation of information concerning grants and fellowships available.

User's Guide to Funding Resources, ed. by Stephen E. Now-
   lan et al. Chilton, 1975. (ISBN 0-8019-6068-1)
   This book is published by Chilton for the Human Resources Network and is intended to help a person find sources
of funds for education, fellowships, scholarships or for a
variety of worthwhile causes. It is arranged by the type of
funding desired and then by national, regional, state and local
sources. For each source, a description of the aid is given,
plus the requirements and limitations on the grant as well
as information concerning how and to whom one should apply.

FICTIONAL CHARACTERS
see
BOOKS - PLOTS AND CHARACTERS

FIRE PROTECTION

Fire Protection Handbook, compiled by the National Fire
   Protection Association. The Association. Annual since
   1904.
   This is a standard handbook of methods of fire pre-
vention. It will be helpful to homeowners and building super-
visors but will also be useful to architects and engineering
in planning ship building.

Municipal Yearbook. International City Managers. Annual
   since 1934.

This is an authoritative résumé of activities and statistical data about all American cities. The information is presented in two ways: signed articles dealing with local developments in each field of municipal concern, i.e., taxes, fire, police, etc., followed by statistical tables giving information on individual cities. There is a directory of all major municipal employees for each city and a good bibliography on municipal problems.

FIRSTS
see
FACTS

FISH*

Fishes of the World; an Illustrated Dictionary, by Alwyne Wheeler. Macmillan, 1975. (ISBN 0-02-626180-4)
Although labeled a dictionary, this is a much more impressive and useful book than that title would indicate. The first section consists of 501 color plates of the various families of fishes and each one is coded with numbers referring to the textual portion of the book. The second part is a dictionary arrangement of the various fishes of the world, often accompanied by black and white drawings to illustrate specific points. Unfortunately, the entries in this section are primarily by the scientific name of the fish rather than the popular name, but there are good cross-references from the common name. Its arrangement limits its usefulness but it is a valuable book if you know the fish you are looking for.

FLAGS*

Flags through the Ages and Across the World, by Whitney Smith. McGraw-Hill, 1975. (ISBN 0-07-059093-1)
A definitive history of world flags from the earliest days to those now waving over the United Nations Plaza. It illustrates in full color and describes in vivid language the flags of the world. Although it is primarily for national standards and is particularly good for description and history

of those flags, it is also one of the very few places that one can find flags of other international organizations such as SEATO, NATO, OAS and others. It is also useful because it has a section, well illustrated, which is devoted to animals and symbols used in heraldry as well as in sports and industry. Surprisingly, the book has one major weakness: it does not cover the flags of the individual states of the United States. In every other respect it is possibly the best book available on flags, symbols, etc. and I would recommend it for inclusion in every library.

American Symbols: The Seals and Flags of the Fifty States, by Henry Hatton. Public Affairs Press, 1974. (ISBN 0-8183-0128-7)
This book corrects the one fatal weakness in the Smith book above; it describes not only the flags but also the seals of the various states. In addition, it includes a good description and history of the national flag and seal.

FOLKLORE*

Encyclopedia of Black Folklore and Humor, by Henry D. Spalding. Jonathan David, 1972. (ISBN 0-8246-0129-7)
This is an excellent book with a collection of almost 2000 folktales, jokes, songs and rhymes from black history. There are even recipes for "soul-food." The one serious flaw is the index, which is unsuitable for a book of this importance.

FOODS*

Calories and Carbohydrates, by Barbara Kraus. Grosset and Dunlap, 1970. (ISBN 0-448-01982-5)
This is an alphabetical listing of various foods by both generic and trade name; for each one the caloric count and carbohydrate content is given. A weight watcher's table.

Larousse Gastronomique: The Encyclopedia of Food, Wine and Cooking, ed. by Charlotte Turgeon and Nina Froud. Crown, 1961. (ISBN 0-517-50333-6)
Eight thousand five hundred recipes, plus an alphabeti-

cal listing of all types of foods, wines and cooking terms make this possibly the best source of information on food currently available.

FOOTBALL*

Football Quizbook, by Al Goldberg. Drake, 1975. (ISBN 0-8473-1105-8)
This is trivia, but the sort that is especially appeal-ing to the true football fan. It will answer those pesky ques-tions about who ran the wrong way in the Rose Bowl game or who was the Galloping Ghost, as well as giving a good deal of background to the history of the sport.

Illustrated Football Rules, by David M. Nelson. Doubleday, 1976. (ISBN 0-385-11406-0)
With TV bringing football into even unwilling living rooms, it helps to understand the rules; this book makes it easier. Each rule is listed, discussed and illustrated by examples of infractions that may occur. An appendix illus-trates the meaning of various signals given by referees.

Football Register. Sporting News. Annual.
This is an annual publication of Sporting News maga-zine, devoted to the players and coaches of professional foot-ball. It is published in late August or early September each year and gives the latest available statistics on all active or recently retired players. It is arranged alphabetically and for each person the usual sporting information is given, such as college attended, honors received, age, weight and posi-tion, as well as statistics of yards gained, tackles made, etc.

FOREIGN WORDS AND PHRASES*

Any good unabridged dictionary will include the more common foreign words and phrases which appear regularly in writing or conversation, but the following book does more than that.

Dictionary of Foreign Terms, by C. O. S. Mawson. 2nd ed. Crowell, 1975. (ISBN 0-690-00171-1)

This includes words from both ancient and modern languages which appear in literary use today. Each word or term is defined and the language identified. If a quote is used, generally the source is given.

FORGERIES - LITERARY

Handy-Book of Literary Curiosities, by William Shepard
    Walsh. Gale, 1966. (Reprint of 1892 ed.) (ISBN 0-
    8103-0162-8)
    Literary curiosities encompass a wide range of topics including but not limited to plagiarism, forgeries, puns, riddles and miscellaneous trivia. Excellent for finding little known literary facts not easily located elsewhere.

Two other books dealing specifically with literary forgeries are:

The History and Motives of Literary Forgeries, by Edmund
    K. Chambers. Burt Franklin, 1968. (Reprint of 1891
    ed.) (ISBN 0-8337-0522-9)

Literary Forgeries, by James A. Farrer. Gale, 1969.
    (Reprint of 1902 ed.) (ISBN 0-8103-3305-8)

FORMS OF ADDRESS

For general use and to answer ninety per cent of your questions on forms of address, a good book of etiquette or protocol will be sufficient. I am listing here the two I feel are best. Also listed is a book dealing entirely with the subject and with titles of nobility as well as the more common variety. It gives the proper forms for both oral and written communication.

The New Emily Post's Etiquette, by Elizabeth L. Post.
    Funk and Wagnalls, 1975. (ISBN 0-308-10167-7)
    The new generation takes over but the legendary Emily Post's daughter maintains the same high standards for protocol and etiquette as her mother. Forms of address can be found in the index under "address--forms of" and will be satisfactory for most of your questions.

Practical Protocol: A Guide to International Courtesies, by
     James E. Lott. Gulf Publications, 1973. (ISBN 0-
     87201-746-X)
          Excellent source for diplomatic and military titles.

Titles and Forms of Address: A Guide to Their Correct Use,
     by J. O. Thorne. 12th ed. St. Martin's Press, 1964.
          Excellent for titles of royalty and government.

FORMULAS, CHEMICAL*

The Formula Book, by Norman Stark. Sheed, 1975. (ISBN
     0-8362-0629-0)

The Formula Book II, by Norman Stark. Sheed, 1976.
     (ISBN 0-8362-0675-4)
          There has not been a really good how-to-do-it book
of formulas and receipts since Henley's Twentieth Century
Book of Formulas went out of print. These books, while
not the equal of the earlier volume, are a good source of
practical advice for the homemaker or handyman. Their
purpose is to provide household chemistry which can be
used to help with home repairs, upkeep and maintenance, as
well as automotive and mechanical problems and personal
appearance. They are especially recommended because they
list where one can expect to find the needed chemicals for
the formula desired--whether the grocery, the drug store or
a chemical supply house. There is a series of useful appendices. Volume one proved so popular that volume two
appeared within the year. Both will prove to be immensely
popular.

FURNITURE*
see
ANTIQUES

GAMES*

Games of the World: How to Make Them, How to Play

Them, How They Came to Be, by Frederick Grunfeld.
Holt, Rinehart & Winston. 1975. (ISBN 0-03-015261-5)
Although only about 80 games are covered in this
book, it is an excellent addition to any library and a worthy
supplement to Hoyle's. It is intended as a history of games
and as an instructional text on making the equipment for those
games, as well as how to play them. It is excellently illustrated.

GASOLINE

Commodity Year Book, ed. by Harry Jiler. Commodity
    Research Bureau, Inc. Annual since 1939.
    This publication gives prices and production statistics
for each of the commodities necessary to the national welfare.
Under "Petroleum," one finds statistics on the world production of petroleum as well as salient statistics on the petroleum industry of the United States. There are summary
statistics for each oil-producing region of the United States
and on oil reserves and probable future uses. There are
charts giving cost of gasoline per gallon in production and
summary charts of gallons of gasoline on hand by month.

Petroleum Facts and Figures. Committee of Public Affairs.
    American Petroleum Institute. Annual since 1928.
    This official annual publication of the American Pe-
troleum Institute is intended to present as much relevant and
valid data as possible concerning the petroleum industry.
It presents, in tabular statistical form, information on production by state and region, refining by state and region and
by type of product, transportation, marketing, prices and
taxation, as well as general information on finances, labor
problems, fires and safety problems, and data for world
production and use. Production and use statistics for gasoline are included, and there is a useful index.

GEMS*

Where to Find What listed several books but they were
primarily on the use of gems in making jewelry. The
books listed below are handbooks intended as guides to the

location and identification of gemstones. In each there are
pictures of various gems as well as instructions on how to
dress the stones for ornamental use.

Gems: Their Sources, Description and Identification, by
　　　Robert Webster. 3rd ed. Archon Books, 1975. (ISBN
　　　0-208-01491-8)

Gemstones and Minerals: A Guide to the Amateur Collector
　　　and Cutter, by Paul Villiard. Winchester Press, 1974.
　　　(ISBN 0-87691-139-4)

GENEALOGY*
see also
PRESIDENTS

American and English Genealogies in the Library of Congress,
　　　compiled by Library of Congress. 2nd ed. Government
　　　Printing Office, 1919. (Reprinted 1967). (ISBN 0-8063-
　　　0349-2)
　　　　　Another excellent search starter. This contains over
7, 000 family names with fine cross-indexing.

The Genealogist's Encyclopedia, by Leslie G. Pine. Wey-
　　　bright & Talley. 1966. (ISBN 0-679-40037-0)
　　　　　A good glossary plus a comprehensive overview of the
problem faced by the genealogist make this an important
book for most libraries.

Heads of Families at the First Census, 1790. 12 vols.
　　　U. S. Bureau of Census. 1907-1909. (Reprint 1964)
　　　Reprint Co. , Spartanburg, S. C.
　　　　　This is a listing of people showing which people with
what names were living in each state and city at the time of
the first census. All the original 13 colonies are included
except Delaware and I don't know why it is missing. This
is a valuable genealogical starting place for most searches.

How to Trace Your Family Tree: A Complete and Easy to
　　　Understand Guide for the Beginner, by the Staff of the
　　　American Genealogical Research Institute. Doubleday,
　　　1975. (ISBN 0-385-09885-5)
　　　　　This is a very small and very inexpensive book, but
a very helpful one for the neophyte genealogist. It can

easily be carried on the search and is good for hints on
places to look as well as ways to do the searching.

GEOGRAPHY*

Gazetteers, compiled by U.S. Department of the Interior.
    Board of Geographic Names. Government Printing Of-
    fice. Published irregularly since 1955. (I 33. 8)
    At present there are 116 gazetteers available from the
Department of the Interior, Board of Geographic Names.
Each one deals with a specific country and gives the names
authorized for use by our government. The Department will
be happy to supply a latest list upon request.

Nicknames and Sobriquets of U. S. Cities and States, by
    Joseph N. Kane and Gerald L. Alexander. 2nd ed.
    Scarecrow Press, 1970. (ISBN 0-8108-0325-9)

Place Names of the World, by Adrian Room. Rowman &
    Littlefield, 1974. (ISBN 0-87471-481-8)
    This is a study of place names, not a gazetteer nor
a geographical guide. It tells the meanings and derivations
of about 1000 names of places around the world. Although
very selective, it is generally excellent for the names included.

GOVERNMENT*

STATE GOVERNMENT

National Directory of State Agencies, compiled by Nancy D.
    Wright and Gene P. Allen. 2nd ed. Herner (Order from
    Information Resources Press), 1976.
    A very comprehensive and reliable listing of the
various agencies of each state government. For each state,
there is a listing of key personnel and agencies. For each
agency there is a discussion of its functions. The book is
divided into two parts. Part one is an alphabetical listing
by states, identifying each agency within the state. Part
two is alphabetical by function, telling which agency in each
state handles that function.

State Administration Officials Classified by Functions. Coun-
    cil of State Governments, 1975. (ISBN 0-87292-013-5)
        This is actually a supplement to The Book of the
States, mentioned in Where to Find What, but it can be purchased separately. It contains a listing of various state
functions arranged alphabetically; for each function there is
a complete listing of the state agency and official handling
it in each state.

LOCAL GOVERNMENT

The County Yearbook: The Authoritative Source Book on
    County Governments, compiled by the National Associa-
    tion of Counties. International City Managers Association.
    Annual, beginning 1975.
        This book is reminiscent of the Municipal Yearbook;
indeed, it is distributed by the same organization. For each
phase of county government it gives an authoritative résumé
of activities and statistical data. There is a directory of all
names and officials of county government as well as activities dealing with specific problems. It is an important book
for all who deal with political questions.

GOVERNMENT BENEFITS

Businessman's Guide to Dealing with the Federal Government.
    Drake, 1973. (ISBN 0-87749-499-1)
        A very brief introduction to the ways to conduct busi-
ness affairs with the U.S. Government. It lists the various
agencies of the government and indicates the possible needs
of each. In addition, there is a section dealing with the ways
to purchase excess government equipment and properties.

Encyclopedia of U.S. Government Benefits, ed. by Roy A.
    Grisham, Jr. and Paul D. McConaughty. 2nd ed. Wise
    and Company, 1975.
        This is a concise presentation of the many services
and benefits offered by the Federal government. Although
concisely presented, the information covers more than 1000
pages of useful information. It is alphabetically arranged by
subject, from aerial photographs to zoological parks. For
each subject there is a discussion of the benefits offered as
well as information as to where and how to obtain additional
information. There are numerous cross-references as well
as an excellent index.

<u>GOVERNMENT PUBLICATIONS</u>*
see also
<u>PERIODICALS</u>

<u>Introduction to United States Public Documents</u>, by Joseph
H. Morehead. Libraries Unlimited, 1975. (ISBN 0-
87287-106-1)
Boyd, Schmeckebier and Rips, move over. There is
a new and, although less comprehensive, much more com-
prehensible book dealing with government documents. This
addition in Libraries Unlimited's <u>Library Science Text Series</u>
is an excellent introduction to the problems of how to or-
ganize and maintain a documents collection as well as a description of the more important series published by the government. Andriot still remains supreme in this last part
but for an easily understood description of the problems of
organization and management, this is the best I've seen.

<u>State Government Reference Publications</u>, by David W. Parish.
Libraries Unlimited, 1974. (ISBN 0-87287-100-2)
This is a guide to almost a thousand official or semi-
official publications which reflect activities of state governments. It is arranged alphabetically by state and can be used
as a basis for book selection for reference materials in the
field.

GOVERNORS - STATE

<u>A Register of the Governors of the States of the United</u>
<u>States of America, 1776-1976</u>, ed. by James J. Gately.
GateFord Publications, 1976.
For the occasions when you have a question about
governors of states other than your own, this will probably
answer your needs. Under each state it gives a chronological list of governors, with dates served, party affiliation and
birth and death dates. It also has an alphabetical list by
governors, repeating the same information, and a final list
that tells which governors were born in one state but became
governor of another. 'Tis a fascinating exercise and may be
of use generally.

GYMNASTICS

Gymnastics Handbook, by Sam Fogel.   Prentice-Hall, 1971.
(ISBN 0-13-371815-8)
Although intended as a high school textbook on gymnastics this is an excellent introduction to various routines
and combinations of activities.   It also has a good section
on the evaluation and scoring of various events by execution
and difficulty.

HANDWRITING ANALYSIS

The Handwriting Analyzer, by Jerome S. Meyer.   Simon &
Schuster, 1953.   (ISBN 0-671-29800-3)
This one is fairly old but it still remains the best
book for parlor parties and home analysis of handwriting.
The format provides transparent but durable paper under
which you can put examples of your handwriting.   In this
way you determine such things as size, slant and character
and then, for each type of letter, there are examples so that
you can pick out characteristics.   All of these various notations are summarized in the final portion of the book and
they often prove quite revealing.   One word to the wise
though: never analyze your mother-in-law's writing; she
will never believe that the book was the source of those
awful things.

HERALDRY*

Heraldic Design, by Heather Child.   Heraldic Book Co.,
1976.   (ISBN 0-8063-0071-X)
This is intended for the beginning student of heraldic
design and includes many sketches and photographs of notable
designs as well as definitions and explanations of essential
rules and laws governing heraldic design.

National Heraldry of the World, by Geoffrey Briggs.   Viking
Press, 1974.   (ISBN 0-670-50452-1)
Although it is fairly easy to find information concern-
ing personal heraldry, this seems to be the first book entire-

devoted to the heraldic arms and devices of individual countries. There are over 100 countries listed and for each there
is a history of the development of the coats of arms and
the date of their origins or changes. For each country
listed, there is a reproduction in color of its arms. The
book is surprisingly up to date, including some countries
which got their beginnings in the current decade.

HERBS *

    Although Where to Find What referred to several
books dealing with the use of herbs, they are found there
either under MEDICINE or FOODS. Users of that book re-
quested that there be a separate section dealing with HERBS.

The Concise Herbal Encyclopedia, by Donald Law. St. Mar-
    tin's Press, 1974.
    The writer of this book has a doctoral degree in the
use of botanical substances in medicine and this book reflects
that interest. It is primarily a book of the use of herbs in
the treatment of both major and minor illnesses. The book
emphasizes that a doctor should be consulted. But in addition to the home treatments described, the book provides a
good historical approach to the subject, telling of the myths
and legendary significance of each herb as well as its medical properties.

A Heritage of Herbs, by Bertha P. Reppert. Stackpole,
    1976. (ISBN 0-8117-0796-2)
    Two hundred and thirty American herbs with full iden-
tification, geographical distribution and possible uses. This
is intended primarily for the home gardener and cook. There
are modernized versions of ancient recipes for both medicinal and nutritional uses.

HIGHWAYS

Highway Statistics, compiled by the U.S. Bureau of Public
    Roads. Government Printing Office. Annual since
    1945. (TD 2.110)
    This presents statistics and tables concerning all

aspects of motor car transportation including motor fuel, driver licensing, highway user taxation, state highway finance and data as well as federal and local highway information. There is a decennial summary of information published in each year ending in 5.

HIKING

The Hiker's Bible, by Robert Elman.   Doubleday, 1973.
(ISBN 0-385-04551-4)
   A comprehensive overview of what it takes to enjoy hiking and backpacking.   It covers hiking techniques and suggests basic and more sophisticated equipment needed for both short and long-distance treks.   It also gives safety hints and location of tracks.   Also of value is a listing of hiking associations and sources of information.   It has a good index.

Introduction to Foot Trails in America, by Robert Colwell.
   Barnes and Noble, 1975.   (ISBN 0-06-465030-8)
   This is divided regionally by Trails East, Trails West, Trails Mid-West and Trails Far West.   For each region there is a listing of the various trails, with information concerning not only the route followed but also the length of the trail, seasons it is open and limitations as to use.   This is an excellent guide to the foot trails of America.   There is a good index.

HOLIDAYS*

Anniversaries and Holidays, by Ruth W. Gregory.   3rd ed.
   American Library Association.   (ISBN 0-8389-0200-6)
   The second edition of this book was listed in Where to Find What but the third edition warrants inclusion in this volume.   It is undoubtedly the best single source of information concerning holidays and it has been expanded and greatly rewritten by an outstanding librarian.   This is a chronological arrangement, first by month and then by days of all the celebrations and anniversaries celebrated in America, but also covering anniversaries from all over the world.   The latest update brings in celebrations which came into being as

late as 1974 in 152 countries. Especially interesting is the section which gives information on possible ways of celebrating each event. There is an excellent index to days by name and a bibliography of more than a thousand items dealing with the history and celebration of various anniversaries and holidays.

Chase's Calendar of Annual Events, Special Days, Weeks and Months. Flint, Michigan: Apple Tree Press. Annual since 1958.

While the information given is quite brief, this little booklet is excellent for finding many holidays and events not listed elsewhere. More than 1,500 days, weeks and events are listed.

HOME REPAIRS
see also
WOODWORKING

Having recently purchased a home, I find that there are many many things which even the amateur can do with proper guidance.

The Good Housekeeping Guide to Fixing Things Around the House, by Marcia D. and Robert M. Liles. Hearst Books, 1974. (ISBN 0-87851-016-8)

This is an omnibus book giving information on all types of necessary repairs around the house. It covers equipment repairs as well as necessary house repairs and for each gives an adequate explanation of the techniques used. The arrangement is partially alphabetical and partially topical, with good cross-references between the two segments, but it would be improved if it had a good index.

The Homeowner's Complete Guide, by Ralph Treves. Dutton, 1974. (ISBN 0-87690-106-2)

This is another in the series of Sunrise Books, each of which has an attractive large format with illustrations as a part of the explanation. It covers not only "how to do it" but also suggests needed tools and explains their proper use. One interesting aspect of the book is a month-by-month calendar of proposed home repairs and maintenance.

Things Your Mother Never Taught You, by Charlotte Slater.

2 vols.   Sheed and Ward, 1974.   (ISBN 0-8362-0552-9)
(IBSN 0-8362-0576-6)
This one is intended for the "liberated" woman but it
is a goldmine of information on everything from changing
flat tires to fixing venetian blinds.   A handy book to have
around whatever your sex.

HOROSCOPES
see
ASTROLOGY

HOUSE PLANTS

There are almost as many books on house plants as
there are house plants; whichever ones I list will bring comments, so I have selected two relatively inexpensive volumes
which I feel are as good as any in the field.

How to Grow House Plants, by The Editors of Sunset Books.
2nd ed.   Lane Publishing Co.   1974.
This slim book gives necessary information concerning
potting, soils, diseases, insects and the many problems that
may arise.   It is well illustrated and has a good plant selection guide.

The World Book of House Plants, by Elvin McDonald.   Rev.
ed.   Funk and Wagnalls, 1975.   (ISBN 0-308-10087-5)
This revised edition of a book first published in 1963
is still a favorite in house-plant circles.   It spends less
time than most such books on the how-to portion (although
covering it adequately) and devotes most of its space to listing specific plants.   For each plant, specific instructions are
given.

HOUSEHOLD HINTS
see
FORMULAS, CHEMICAL

HUMOR

Subject Guide to Humor: Anecdotes, Facetiae, and Satire
from 365 Periodicals, 1968-74, by Jean S. Kujoth.
Scarecrow Press, 1976. (ISBN 0-8108-0924-9)
This will be a great help to you in locating stories
for people making speeches or writing papers and needing
the humorous touch. The listings are by broad subject categories and then alphabetically by authors. There is also a
title listing. Unfortunately, no cartoons are included.

HYPNOTISM

Although there have been many requests for listings
of books on hypnotism, particularly from the how-to-do-it
standpoint, I am resisting the inclination to include some.
Hypnotism is not something that the inexperienced should toy
with; it should only be done by a fully qualified psychologist
and then only rarely. For this reason, I have included one
book which is a summary of the things believed and the things
actually true about hypnotism. It is a popular treatment but
it answers most legitimate questions. There is a good bibliography if further information is desired.

Hypnosis: Fact and Fiction, by Frederick L. Marcuse.
Gannon, 1962. (ISBN 0-88307-400-1)

IDEOGRAMS

Alphabet: A Key to the History of Mankind, by David
Diringer. 2v. Funk and Wagnalls, 1968. (ISBN 0-308-
40036-4)
An excellent history of the development of writing
from the earliest cave painting to the modern day. Part I
is a discussion of all types of ideographic writings.

Forgotten Scripts, by Cyrus H. Gordon. Basic Books, 1968.
(ISBN 0-465-02483-1)
This is basically a book about the discovery of ways
to decipher ancient writings and the effect that these dis-

coveries have had on the study of history. There are excellent pictures and line drawings of various ideograms.

Writing: Man's Great Invention, by J. Hambleton Ober.
    Peabody Institute, 1965. (ISBN 0-8392-1139-2)
    Another excellent history of the development of writing, with chapters on each of the various forerunners in Mesopotamia, Crete, Egypt, Syria and Greece. A beautiful book with excellent charts of all types of ideograms.

ILLITERACY

For current articles and programs for combating illiteracy either of the two major periodical indices in the educational field are excellent sources.

Education Index, a Cumulative Author Subject Index to a
    Selected List of Educational Periodicals... H. W.
    Wilson Company. Quarterly with annual cumulations since 1929.

Current Index to Journals in Education. Macmillan. Monthly
    with annual cumulations since 1969.

For statistics concerning illiteracy:

Standard Education Almanac. Marquis Academic Media.
    Annual since 1967.
    The purpose of this publication is to present the most comprehensive and latest statistics on all aspects of American education. There are charts showing the decrease in illiteracy by both race and sex as well as percentages by geographic location and the percentage of those rejected for military service under the draft.

Statesman's Yearbook: Statistical and Historical Annual of
    All the States of the World. St. Martin's Press. Annual since 1864.
    This is a basic tool for world-wide governmental information. It presents both written and tabular information of all sorts dealing with the governments of the world. For the United States, there is a section for the national government and one for each of the states. For each governmental unit discussed, the following information is given: the ruler,

the constitution and government, area, population, religious statistics, programs of social welfare, justice, education, finances, defense and all other phases of government. It gives a list of major diplomatic representatives to and from each country. There are also bibliographies on each country and a section on the United Nations. This is a must book for any library. It is excellent for the latest literacy statistics.

INCOME TAX*

Although Where to Find What covers the income tax question fairly adequately, there have been several publications recently that may be of interest to libraries and their users.

Clergy's Federal Income Tax Guide, ed. by F. H. Heath. 1976 ed. Abingdon, 1976. Annual.
This is a tax guide prepared specifically to help clergymen prepare their own returns.

Farmer's Tax Guide, published by U.S. Internal Revenue Service. Government Printing Office. Annual since 1944. (T22. 44)
Special tax rules for income and self employment for farmers.

Practical Guide to Individual Income Tax Return Preparation, by Sidney Kess and Ben Eisenberg. Commerce Clearing House, 1974.
This is another of the excellent publications of the Commerce Clearing House and discusses almost every aspect that the average person will encounter in the preparation of his tax return. It is written in an easily understood manner and is further simplified by the use of typical situations and their solutions.

Take It Off! More Than One-Thousand Tax Deductions Most People Overlook, by Robert S. Holzman. Crowell, 1976. (ISBN 0-690-01182-2)
Has anyone ever mailed in his/her tax return with the nagging question, "Have I deducted everything to which I am entitled?" Even with this book, you may find yourself still wondering, but it lists almost all legal deductions as well as

giving documentation from the Internal Revenue Code as to
their legality. It is easily read and understood.

INDIANS*

American Indians, 1492-1975: A Chronology and Fact Book,
ed. by Henry C. Dennis. Oceana Publ., 1976. (ISBN
0-379-00526-3)
While not definitive and presenting only a base outline
of Indian history, this lists chronologically most of the important events of Indian history after the arrival of the white
man.

Biographical Sketches and Anecdotes of 95 to 120 Principal
Chiefs from the Indian Tribes of North America, edited
by Thomas L. McKenney and James Hall. U.S. Bureau
of Indian Affairs, Government Printing Office, 1967.
(I 20.2: In 2/27)
This is a reprint of a document printed in 1838 but it
is still excellent for physical descriptions of Indian Chiefs
and little-known biographical data.

Handbook of South American Indians, ed. by Julian H. Stew-
ard. 7 vols. Smithsonian Institution. Bureau of American Ethnology. Government Printing Office, 1959.
(SI 2.3:143)
This, probably the best source of information concerning the Indians of South America, was published as Bulletin
#143 of the Bureau of American Ethnology. It contains a
descriptive list of all the major tribal groups as well as information on their life and history.

INSIGNIA

American Badges and Insignia, by Evans E. Kerrigan.
Viking Press, 1967. (ISBN 0-670-11702-1)

American War Medals and Decorations, by Evans E. Kerrigan. Viking Press, 1971. (ISBN 0-670-12101-0)
Together these two books provide a comprehensive
guide to all military badges and insignia worn by the United

States Armed Forces. Each badge or insignia is pictured
in black and white and described fully in the accompanying
text.   There are 1, 100 black and white illustrations and
eight plates showing 100 ribbons in full color.

Heraldry and Regalia of War, ed. by Bernard Fitzsimons.
    Beckman House, 1973.   (ISBN 0-517-130866)
    This is a worldwide collection of the insignia of the
Armed Forces.   Uniforms, ribbons, insignia and badges are
illustrated often in full color.

INSURANCE AND INSURANCE COMPANIES *

Life and Health Insurance Handbook, ed. by Davis W. Gregg
    and Vane B. Lucas.   3rd ed.   Dow-Jones Irwin, 1973.
    (ISBN 0-87094-063-5)
    This is written primarily for the insurance salesman
but will be helpful to anyone interested in the subject.   It
covers all major aspects of the insurance program including
pensions, profit sharing, annuities and estate planning.   It
offers particularly good explanations via charts, tables and
diagrams, contracts and forms used in the industry.

State Administrative Officials Classified by Function.   The
    Council of State Governments, 1975.   (ISBN 0-87292-013-
    5)
    This is a supplement to the Book of the States men-
tioned in Where to Find What.   Under the heading INSURANCE
you will find a listing of agencies and officials in each state
handling this subject.

INTEREST

        There is a very good discussion and explanation of
interest and its effect on amounts paid in the following books:

Sylvia Porter's Money Book, by Sylvia Porter.   Rev. ed.
    Doubleday, 1976.   (ISBN 0-385-12612-3)
    The subtitle of this book is "How to earn it, spend
it, save it, invest it, borrow it and use it to better your
life."   Written by an outstanding newspaper writer on personal

finance, this book is as good a discussion of home budgets
and budgetary problems as I have seen. It covers almost
any conceivable fiscal problem that will face a family and
discusses it in easily understood language. I could think of
no better wedding present for any couple.

For tables showing interest schedules see:

The Thorndike Encyclopedia of Banking and Financial Tables,
    by David Thorndike. Warren, Gordon & Lamont, 1974.
    (ISBN 0-88262-062-2)
    This book contains tables for real estate, depreciation,
compound interest, annuity interest, savings, installment
loans, rebates, mortgage values and stock yields. There
are tables to show every possible combination of percentages
and years to be calculated. This book will answer quickly
most of your financial statistical questions.

INTERNATIONAL LANGUAGES
see
LANGUAGES, INTERNATIONAL

INTERNATIONAL STANDARD BOOK NUMBERS
(ISBN)

Books in Print. R. R. Bowker, annual. 4 vols.
Publishers' Trade List Annual. R. R. Bowker, annual.
    6 vols.
Subject Guide to Books in Print. R. R. Bowker, annual.
    2 vols.
    The three publications, while separates, should still
be considered as a unit. The three together provide an
accurate, easily used and understood bibliography of publications currently available in the United States. The Publishers' Trade List Annual is a compilation of publishers' catalogs bound in a uniform set. It does not contain every publisher but comes as close as is possible. Books in Print
was formerly an index to the PTLA but now provides the
price, publisher, author and ISBN number for almost every
book currently in print. The Subject Guide is useful in cases
where you are searching not for a specific book but for books
on a specific subject.

For books not yet published, check:

Forthcoming Books, Now Including New Books in Print. R.
    R. Bowker. 6 times per year.
    This might be considered a supplement to the above-
listed books since it contains publishers' forecasts of their
output for five months in advance. It gives the same bibliographic data found in the permanent volumes.

INTERNATIONAL STANDARD SERIAL NUMBERS
(ISSN)

Ulrich's International Periodicals Directory, A Classified
    Guide to Current Periodicals, Foreign and Domestic.
    R. R. Bowker. Published in alternating years.
    This is a classified listing of the world's periodical
publications. For each periodical the usual information is
given: publisher, editor, place of publication, price of sub-
scription, total circulation, and places that the periodical is
indexed. It contains all the information listed in the Standard
Periodical Directory but in a much more pleasing format.
There is a numerical listing telling to whom each ISSN is
assigned.

INVENTIONS *

Dictionary of Inventions and Discoveries, by E. F. Carter.
    2nd ed. Crane Russak, 1976. (ISBN 0-8448-0867-9)
    An alphabetical listing of thousands of inventions and
scientific developments since the invention of the wheel. For
each invention is given its name and the year of invention if
known. The book lacks some credibility since no source is
cited for the information, but it presents concise identification and dating as a good way to start searching.

Eureka! An Illustrated History of Inventions from the Wheel
    to the Computer, ed. by Edward DeBono. Holt, Rine-
    hart & Winston. 1974. (ISBN 0-03-012641-X)
    This one is fully documented with signed articles writ-
ten in non-technical language. There are many photographs,
drawings and charts. The arrangement is a trifle difficult

in that it is first by broad subject categories and then chronological, making the use of the index imperative.

JEWISH PEOPLE*

A History of Judaism, by Daniel J. Silver and Bernard
     Martin. 2 vols. Basic Books, 1976. (ISBN 0-465-
     03004-1) (ISBN 0-465-03005-X)
     This two-volume history of the Jewish people will not
replace the magnificent 14-volume set written by Salo W.
Baron since that is the standard by which all such histories
must be judged. On the other hand, this one is much more
likely to be read in its entirety. The very size of Baron
frightens most persons but this set is well written and has
an excellent format; both aesthetically and intellectually, it
is a pleasure.

JOURNALISTS

The Working Press of the Nation, ed. by Milton Paule.   5
     vols. Working Press, 1976.
     This basic book provides reliable and up-to-date in-
formation on almost 1000 feature writers and over 3000
magazines of this country. The price, combined with its
annual schedule, puts it out of the range of the smaller library but it should certainly be on the shelves of every
college library and all but the smallest public libraries.

KINGS AND RULERS*

Kings and Queens of England, by Eric R. Delderfield.   Rev.
     ed. Stein and Day, 1972. (ISBN 0-8128-1493-2)
     This is a basic book for the study of British Royalty.
It lists and gives a brief discussion of the reign of each English monarch from the earliest to the modern queen.   For
each reign, the dates of beginning and ending as well as a
listing of principal events are given.

KNIVES

There are two types of questions about knives which most often confront the reference librarian. The first category is questions concerning the history and the development of various types of cutlery and tableware from the stone knife to present-day silverware. Unfortunately, there are no titles currently in print on this aspect of the subject. One useful out-of-print item is:

The Story of Cutlery, by J. B. Himsworth. John DeGraff, 1953. o. p.

The other aspect is the knife as a tool or a weapon and there are many books available in this area. The best are listed below:

American Knives, by Harold L. Peterson. Scribner, 1958. (ISBN 0-684-10462-8)
A history of the knives that made American history from the frontier days to World War II.

Knives and Edged Weapons, edited by Jim Woods. Peterson Publications. (ISBN 0-8227-0054-9)
A history and description of edged weapons of the world. Well illustrated.

KNOTS *

Handbook of Knots and Splices, by Charles E. Gibson. Emerson Books. 1976. (ISBN 0-87523-146-2)
A very easily understood descriptive book on rope tying. It tells how to select the rope you need for the knot you want and gives step-by-step instructions. In addition to knots, it describes splicing and braiding techniques. Fine drawings aid in understanding.

LABOR AND LABOR UNIONS *

Biographical Dictionary of American Labor Leaders, ed. by

Gary M. Fink and Milton Cantor. Greenwood Press, 1974. (ISBN 0-8371-7643-3)

This is the usual who's who-type publication on leaders in the field of labor. For each of 500 personalities are given the important facts and dates. Although most of the persons covered are current leaders, there are some from the early period of labor organization in this country. There are six appendixes which list such interesting aspects as length of education, religion, union affiliation, political party, date of birth and public office held.

Labor Reference Book, by Adrian A. Paradis. Chilton, 1972. (ISBN 0-8019-5727-3)

This is an alphabetical listing of the most important words and concepts of the labor movement. It includes, in addition to definitions, listings and biographical sketches of many famous labor leaders and some manufacturers who have influenced the labor movement. Excellent for quick reference and a guide to further study.

State Administrative Officials Classified by Function. Council of State Governments, 1975. (ISBN 0-87292-013-5)

This is a supplement to The Book of the States mentioned in Where to Find What. Under the heading LABOR, you will find a listing of relevant agencies and officials in each state.

LANGUAGE, ARTIFICIAL
see
LANGUAGE, INTERNATIONAL

LANGUAGE, INTERNATIONAL

There have been many attempts to develop an artificial or universal language and every good encyclopedia has articles dealing with these attempts and their success or failure. Listed here are books describing the more important attempts.

Currently the most highly regarded of the artificial languages is Interlingua developed by the International Auxiliary Language Association. It takes word forms commonly occurring in the major Western languages and creates a language which almost anyone in Europe or America can easily read.

Interlingua at Sight, by Alexander Gode.   Ungar, 1961.
(ISBN 0-8044-0188-8)

   The other artificial language which has gained fairly
wide acceptance is Esperanto.

Teach Yourself Esperanto, by John Cresswell and John Hart-
ley.   McKay.   (ISBN 0-679-10167-5)

Esperanto-English Dictionary, by M. C. Butler.   2 vols.
Esperanto Books, 1967.
   Then there is a very good discussion of the whole
philosophy and need for an international language.   It gives
a brief summary of each one and examples of problems
caused both domestically and internationally by a failure to
communicate.   It is written by one of the foremost philolo-
gists of our time:

One Language For the World, by Mario Pei.   Devin-Adair,
1969.   (ISBN 0-8159-6403-X)

LAST WORDS

   Almost every book of quotations has a listing of
famous last words, but they are generally so scattered that
they are difficult to find.   There are a multitude of dictionaries of last words and three are listed here in descending
order of preference by the writer.

The Last Words of Distinguished Men and Women, by F. R.
Marvin.   Gordon Press.   (ISBN 0-8490-0488-8)

Last Words of Saints and Sinners, ed. by Herbert Lockyer.
Rev. ed.   Kregel, 1975.   (ISBN 0-8254-3111-5)

Last Words of Famous Men, by Bega.   Folcroft, 1973 (reprint of 1930 ed.).

LAW ENFORCEMENT
see also
POLICE

FEDERAL

Annual Report of the National Institute of Law Enforcement
and Criminal Justice, issued by U.S. Department of
Justice. Government Printing Office. Annual since
1974. (J1. 1/3)
Covers the activities of the Justice Department's Law
Enforcement Division for the previous year.

Uniform Crime Report, issued by Federal Bureau of Investi-
gation. Government Printing Office. Annual since 1930.
This presents in one volume the annual statistical
data on crime trends, crime rates and statistics for cities
of 25, 000, as well as police employment data, persons ar-
rested, persons cleared and a classification of offenses.
Good statistical charts.

STATE

The Book of the States. Published by the Council of State
Governments. Biennial since 1935.
This is a comprehensive guide to state governments.
For each state there is a directory of officials, general information and statistics, and many articles dealing with the
problems and recent developments of state governments in
the past biennium. There is an excellent account of public
safety activities each year.

State Administrative Officials Classified by Function. Council of State Governments, 1975. (ISBN 0-87292-013-5)
This is a special supplement to the Book of the States.
Under the heading LAW ENFORCEMENT you will find a listing of appropriate agencies and officials in each state.

Municipal Yearbook. International City Managers. Annual
since 1934.
This is an authoritative résumé of activities and statistical data about all American cities. The information is
presented in two ways: signed articles dealing with local
developments in each field of municipal concern, i.e., taxes,
fire, police, etc., followed by statistical tables giving information on individual cities. There is a directory of all
major municipal employees for each city and a good bibliography on municipal problems.

LAWNS

Lawn Keeping, by Robert W. Schery.   Prentice-Hall, 1976.
   (ISBN 0-13-526889-3)
      This is an excellent guide to a good lawn.   It pro-
vides complete instructions and explains the why's as well as
the how's of lawn care.

LEGAL TERMS*

Black's Law Dictionary, by Henry Campbell Black.   4th ed.
   West Publishing Company, 1968.
      This is the standard legal dictionary for terms and
phrases found in either American or British Law.   All terms
are defined and pronunciations given.   This book has been
constantly in print since 1891, so its authority is unquestioned.

Law Dictionary of Practical Definitions, by Edward J. Bander.
   Oceana Publications, 1966.   (ISBN 0-379-11058-X)
      This volume in the Oceana Law Library gives defini-
tions of law terms in everyday language.   Not for the professional, it will nevertheless answer most questions.

LEGISLATION

      For a summary of current legislation there are a
multitude of sources and information:

Congressional Record.   Government Printing Office.   Daily
   while Congress is in session since 1873.   (X181.)
      This daily accounting of the happenings in Congress
constitutes a complete history of all legislation.   Sometimes
the texts of the bills are included but normally they are referred to only by names and subjects.   The set is cumulated
annually and recently has become available in various micro-
forms.

Facts on File, a Weekly World News Digest with a Cumulative Index.   Facts on File.   Annual cumulations since
   1940.

This is a weekly publication of news events with bi-weekly indexes. Excellent for recent legislation actions.

Congressional Quarterly Weekly Report. Congressional
    Quarterly, Inc. Weekly with annual cumulations since
    1941.
    There is a summary chart of general legislative
activity for each week, giving a list of bills and actions taken
and special reports on all aspects of the legislative program
and other important government happenings.

LITERATURE*

POETRY

Poetry Handbook: A Dictionary of Terms, by Babette
    Deutsch. 4th ed. Funk and Wagnalls, 1974. (ISBN
    0-308-10088-3)
    This is the standard dictionary of poetic terms and
describes forms of poetry and poetic expression. It covers
from the pre-Christian to the modern era. Definitions are
usually accompanied with illustrations of use. This is a
book which should be in every academic or school library.

WORLD LITERATURE

Cassell's Encyclopedia of World Literature, ed. by John
    Buchanan-Brown. Rev. ed. 3 vols. Morrow, 1973.
    (ISBN 0-688-00228-5)
    This is an updated and revised edition of an excellent
work which first appeared in 1953. The first volume consists
of essays dealing with a variety of literary subjects, and
volumes 2 and 3 are biographies of literary figures from the
classics to the modern day. All articles are signed by
scholars in the field. It is a book which can be highly recommended for all but the smallest libraries.

LOTTERIES

Readers' Guide to Periodical Literature. H. W. Wilson
    Co. Semi-monthly with annual cumulations since 1900.

Since the discussion of legal lotteries is still quite current, most of the best information will be found by consulting periodicals.

Congressional Quarterly Weekly Report. Congressional
    Quarterly, Inc. Weekly with annual cumulations since
    1941.
        This is a summary of general legislative activity
for each week, giving a listing of bills acted upon and actions
taken. There are often special reports on all aspects of the
legislative program and other important government happenings.

Editorial Research Reports. Published by Congressional
    Quarterly, Inc. Weekly with annual cumulations since
    1963.
        Each week there is an Editorial Research report
issued dealing with recent legislative or social happenings.
There have been several dealings with lotteries but the most
recent is called "Gambling in America" and appeared on
March 8, 1972 (Vol. I, pp. 193-210).

State Administrative Officials Classified by Functions. Coun-
    cil of State Governments, 1975. (ISBN 0-87292-013-5)
        This is a supplement to The Book of the States.
Under the heading LOTTERIES you will find a listing of relevant officials and agencies for each state.

State-Conducted Lotteries. Hearing Before the Sub-Committee
    on Claims and Government Relations of the Judiciary
    Committee. U.S. House of Representatives. Govern-
    ment Printing Office. (Y4 J89. 1:93-46)
        This is a hearing which summarizes the arguments
pro and con concerning state-sponsored lotteries and the way
their sponsors hope they will curb illicit gambling and provide needed revenue. There are photostats of ads for five
state lotteries.

MACHINE TOOLS
see
POWER TOOLS

MAGIC*

The Amateur Magician's Handbook, by Henry Hay.   3rd rev.
    ed.   Crowell, 1972.   (ISBN 0-690-05711-3)
    Aimed at the amateur, this book has been proclaimed
by the professional.   Each trick is amply illustrated and explained.   Tricks run from simple card tricks to the latest
in mental magic.

The Handbook of Mental Magic, by Marvin Kaye.   Stein and
    Day, 1975.   (ISBN 0-8128-1818-0)
    This is a rather specialized book on magic, dealing
entirely with the field of mental magic, i.e., hypnotism,
mind reading, etc., but it is an excellent book on this specific aspect of the field and is complemented by an excellent
glossary as well as an annotated bibliography of related materials.   Particularly of value to the amateur is the listing
of magic equipment supply houses.

MAPS
see
UNITED STATES - ATLASES; RELIGION - ATLAS

MEDICAL PROFESSION

American Medical Directory.   American Medical Association.
    Biennial since 1906.
    This is a register of all the members of the Ameri-
can Medical Association in the United States and Canada.   In
addition to its strictly biographical function it contains information about the American Medical Association, medical
schools and a geographical arrangement of doctors.

Directory of Medical Specialists.   17th ed.   2 vols.   A. N.
    Marquis Co. 1975.   (ISBN 0-8379-0517-6)
    A listing of physicians who have official specialties.
For each the usual biographical data, i.e., birth, education,
marital status, are given.   There is an alphabetical list of
doctors, a list by specialties and a geographic list.

MEDICARE

Medicare and Social Security Explained, ed. by CCH Editorial Staff. Chicago, Ill.: Commerce Clearing House, 1970.
This is a handy compilation of pertinent data on Federal Old Age benefits, covering not only Social Security but
also medicare, survivor's and disability benefits, and related programs. It is aided by a topical index. This seems
to be the best non-governmental publication on the subject.

Directory, Medicare Providers and Suppliers of Services,
published by U. S. Social Security. Government Printing
Office. Annual since 1967.
The services for all agencies eligible for medical uses
are listed here: Home Health Agencies, Hospitals, Extended
Care Facilities, Independent laboratories and Out-patient
Physical Therapy.

Directory of Home Health Agencies Certified as Medicare
Providers, compiled by Council of Home Health Agencies.
National League of Nursing, 1975.

METRIC SYSTEM

Slowly but surely the United States edges its way to-
ward an acceptance of the metric system of measurement, and
libraries need to be prepared for more questions.

Think Metric Now! A Step-by-Step Guide to Understanding
and Applying the Metric System, by Paul J. Hartsuch.
Follett, 1974. (ISBN 0-695-80449-9)
The title adequately describes both the mission and
the contents of this book. Although short, it discusses each
type of metric measurement and then presents tests so that
the user can determine if he has mastered the program.

MILITARY LEADERS

World Military Leaders, ed. by Paul Martell and Grace P.
Hayes. Bowker, 1974. (ISBN 0-8352-0785-4)

This is a companion volume to Bowker's Almanac
of World Military Power and gives biographical data on the
major and some minor military leaders of 117 countries.
More than 2000 military leaders are listed.   Emphasis of the
biographical sketches is military, but other important posts
are listed.

MINERALOGY*

Minerals of the World: A Field Guide and Introduction to
the Geology and Chemistry of Minerals, by Charles A.
Sorrell.   Golden Press.   1974.   (ISBN 0-307-47005-9)
This is an intermediate book, not for the beginner but
for the person already acquainted with the subject.   It arranges several hundred minerals by class and then gives the
physical or chemical qualities of each.   It is excellent for
crystallography but because of its arrangement, must be used
by the beginner in connection with other books.

Treasures from the Earth: The World of Rocks and Minerals,
by Benjamin Shaub.   Crown Publishers, 1975.   (ISBN
0-517-52347-7)
This one is for the beginning collector of minerals.
It discusses the elementary aspects of crystallography and
the various physical qualities of minerals.   There are descriptions of many types of minerals and information on
where to find them.

MISSIONS

Two aspects of this subject are the physical buildings
and the missionary efforts of the various churches.

MISSIONARY EFFORTS

Mission Handbook: North American Protestant Ministries
Overseas, prepared by the Mission Research Library
and edited by Edward R. Dayton.   10th ed.   Missions
Advanced Research and Communications Center, Monro-
via, Calif., 1973.   (ISBN 0-912552-03-4)
The book is in two parts.   Part one is a series of
essays which analyze the place that missions play in a modern

society and the means of financing and staffing them. The rest of the book is based on statistical data derived from a questionnaire sent to all Protestant churches and answers the questions of how many missions and missionaries there are, what they do and how they do it.

Official Catholic Directory. J. P. Kenedy & Sons. Annual since 1886.
    This official publication is an annual directory of all members of the Catholic hierarchy in the United States. It lists Catholic missionaries and missions.

MISSIONS BUILDINGS

Early 17th Century Missions of the South West, by Francis Parsons. King, 1975. (ISBN 0-912762-21-7)

Guide Book to the Missions of California, by Marjorie Camphause. Ward Ritchie Press, 1974. (ISBN 0-378-03792-7)
    This is a brief tourist handbook which describes the California missions and the men who founded them. Excellent for the purpose intended.

Missions and Missionaries of California, by Zephyrin Engelhardt. 4 vols. Milford House, 1974. (ISBN 0-87821-019-9)

MORTGAGE

There is a very good discussion and chart of mortgage payments in the following book:

Sylvia Porter's Money Book, by Sylvia Porter. Doubleday, 1975. (ISBN 0-385-08484-6)
    The subtitle of this book is "How to earn it, spend it, save it, invest it, borrow it and use it to better your life." Written by an outstanding newspaper writer on personal finance, this book is as good a discussion of home budgets and budgetary problems as I have seen. It covers almost any conceivable fiscal problem that will face a family and discusses it in easily understood language.

Savings and Loan Financing Sourcebook, published by U.S. Federal Home Loan Bank Board. Government Printing Office. Annual since 1952. (FHL 1.11)

Includes data on interest rates, mortgage activity and construction requirements.

For tables showing mortgage schedules see:

The Thorndike Encyclopedia of Banking and Financial Tables, by David Thorndike. Warren, Gorham & Lamont, 1974. (ISBN 0-88262-062-2)

This book contains tables for real estate, depreciation, compound interest, annuity interest, savings, installment loans, rebates, mortgage values and stock yields. There are tables to show every possible combination of percentages and years to be calculated. This book will answer quickly most of your financial statistical questions.

MOTHS

The Dictionary of Butterflies and Moths in Color, by Alan Watson and Paul E. S. Whalley. McGraw-Hill, 1975. (ISBN 0-07-068490-1)

A beautiful and very useful book, this has 405 photographs in color as well as an alphabetical index to the moths and butterflies of the world. More than 2000 are listed and described. There is a glossary of terms used as well as a good bibliography.

The Moth Book, a Popular Guide to the Knowledge of the Moths of North America, by W. J. Holland. Dover Publ. rev. ed. 1968. (ISBN 0-486-21948-8)

In 1903, W. J. Holland wrote this book and it has remained the book on the subject since that time. This is a revised edition published in 1968 and edited by A. E. Brower, himself a recognized authority in the field. Although old, the book still remains the chief reference source for amateur lepidopterists and Dr. Brower has updated and corrected the earlier book in the light of recent scientific discoveries. For each type of moth there is a complete description with pictures and identification data. In addition, there is an introductory chapter which gives a life history of the moth. Although most of the pictures are in black and white, there are 48 color plates showing most of the common moths of North America. In all more than 10,000 species are identified.

MOTOR VEHICLE REGISTRATION

Digest of Motor Laws, compiled by Cornelius R. Gray.
　　Falls Church, Virginia: American Automobile Associa-
　　tion. Annual.
　　　This is a summary of regulations governing registration and operation of passenger cars in the United States,
the Canal Zone, Guam, Puerto Rico, the Virgin Islands and
the Provinces of Canada. Compiled by the legal department
of the American Automobile Association.

State Administration Officials Classified By Functions.
　　Council of State Governments, 1975. (ISBN 0-87292-013-
　　5)
　　　This is a supplement to the Book of the States mentioned in Where to Find What. Under the heading MOTOR
VEHICLES* - REGISTRATION you will find a listing of
agencies and officials in each state.

Highway Statistics. Compiled by the U. S. Bureau of Public
　　Roads. Government Printing Office. Annual since 1945.
　　(TD2. 110)
　　　This presents statistics and tables concerning all aspects of motor car transportation including motor fuel, driver licensing, highway taxation, state financing and state data
as well as federal and local highway information. There is
a decennial summary of information published in each year
ending in a 5.

MUSEUMS*

　　Where to Find What listed the Official Museum Directory which is a directory of museums of the United States
and Canada. The book listed below is worldwide in scope.

The Directory of World Museums, ed. by Kenneth Hudson
　　and Ann Nicholls. Columbia, 1975. (ISBN 0-231-03907-
　　7)
　　　Twenty-two thousand museums around the world are
listed, giving the name of the director, the name of the
museum and its speciality and address, as well as a brief
description of the various collections and the hours the museum or art gallery is open. It is arranged geographically

by country and then by city within the country. Appendixes
include a classified list of subjects covered as well as a
glossary of terms used.

Aviation and Space Museums of America, by Jon Allen.
    Arco, 1975. (ISBN 0-668-03426-2)
    With an ever-increasing interest in space technology,
a directory of aviation and space museums becomes more
important each year. This one will be helpful not only to
the aviation or space buff but to the casual traveler as well.
It tells what types of things can be found in each museum,
its location, its hours and admission charges if any.

MUSHROOMS

Complete Book of Mushrooms; Over 1000 Species and Varie-
    ties of American, European and Asiatic Mushrooms with
    460 Illustrations in Black and White and in Color, by
    Augusto Rinaldi and Vassili Tyndalo. Crown Publishers,
    1974. (ISBN 0-517-51493-1)
    Although an Italian publication, this book identifies the
mushrooms of North America as well as those from other
parts of the world. It identifies and describes over 1000
varieties and has pictures of more than 600 of these; many
in color. Pictures of mushrooms are sometimes misleading
because a single variety may have several different shadings,
but the textual description elaborates on the pictured variety
and tells of possible variations in colors. In addition, there
is a full description of the size, odor, cap and stem and
other physical features. Importantly, it identifies whether
each variety is poisonous or not. It also gives the times of
the year at which each variety thrives.

    The above is possibly the most complete book avail-
able for the amateur mushroom collector but it should be
used in connection with the following, which has long been the
standard field guide to North American collectors:

Mushroom Hunter's Field Guide, by Alexander H. Smith.
    Rev. and enlarged. University of Michigan, 1963.
    (ISBN 0-472-85609-X)

The Mushroom Pocket Field Guide, by Howard E. Bigelow.
    Macmillan, 1974. (ISBN 0-02-51065-3)

This is not as complete as either of the other two titles above, but it is intended as a field guide. It limits its coverage to the 60 types of fungi found in North America. It is a handy guide for beginners but less easily used than the Smith book.

Mushrooms of North America, by Orson K. Miller. Dutton, 1972. (ISBN 0-525-16165-1)
Literally an encyclopedia of mushroom lore, it describes and illustrates nearly 700 species of mushrooms found in the United States and Canada. There is a general discussion of poisonous and non-poisonous mushrooms and hints on the best ways to cook and serve the latter. Excellent pictorial keys and color plates aid in ready identification. Of all the books listed, this is probably the best for the beginning collector.

MUSIC AND MUSICIANS*

The Dictionary of Contemporary Music, edited by John Vinton. Dutton, 1974. (ISBN 0-525-09125-4)
The contemporary music of the title is mostly concert music but, within that limitation, this is an excellent work. It is in handbook form, in one alphabet covering biographies of composers, types of music, national developments and definitions of terms. There are more than 1000 articles, most of which are signed. This is an excellent source for almost any aspect of contemporary concert music.

New Oxford History of Music. J. A. Westrup, et al., eds. Oxford University Press, 1957- .
Like some other Oxford history series, this one is still in the process of completion but promises to be the most important set for the general public in the field of musical history. Volumes one through seven and volume ten have been completed, with the remaining volumes projected within the next two years. It is too expensive a set for the small library but should be available at any nearby university having a department of music.

World Chronology of Music History, by Paul E. Eisler. Oceana Publ. 1972- . (ISBN 0-379-16080-3)
The first three of ten projected volumes of this massive work have been published. Although quite specialized,

it is a book that should be in any library with musical pre-
tentions. It is, as stated, a chronology of musical history
from prehistory down to modern times. The first three
volumes cover up to the 18th century. It is more than a
mere chronology since it discusses the lives and music of
each composer as introduced.

MUSIC - COUNTRY AND WESTERN

Encyclopedia of Folk, Country and Western Music, by Irwin
Stambler and Grelun Landon. St. Martin's Press, 1969.
Although now becoming dated in a field that is changing quickly, this is nevertheless an important work for performers and composers prior to 1970. There are 500 biographies, many with photographs, as well as a good dictionary
of musical terms.

Country Music Encyclopedia, by Melvin Shestack. Crowell,
1974. (ISBN 0-690-00442-7)
While much more restricted than the Stambler book
this brings that book up to date in the field of strictly country music. This book has an alphabetical directory of all
current performers whose credits include appearance in the
top 100 charts as well as more definitive articles on the
superstars. In addition there are biographies of the pioneers
in the field. The volume is well illustrated with many photographs.

Sing Your Heart Out, Country Boy, by Dorothy Horstman.
E. P. Dutton, 1975. (ISBN 0-525-20465-2)
This is a compilation of the lyrics of practically
every important country music song ever written. Compiler
Horstman has a Sunday afternoon radio show on station WNYC
in New York City. Her book is arranged by type of song,
with each lyric introduced by either the composer or the
artist most closely associated with that song. This enables
the reader to gain clearer insight into the background and
meaning of the song. There is an excellent index to song
titles and a bibliography of sources of information on every
major performer. The book should be in every library in
this day of increasing popularity of country and western music.

MUSICAL INSTRUMENTS

A Survey of Musical Instruments, by Sibyl Marcuse. Harper
and Row, 1975. (ISBN 0-06-012776-7)
   This is a very scholarly work and may be more detailed than desired by many libraries but it is the very best
source of historical and technical information concerning the
four classes of instruments. Each instrument is traced from
its most primitive appearance to the present or up to the
time it was superseded by a more modern instrument.

Musical Instruments through the Ages, ed. by Anthony Baines.
Walker, 1975. (ISBN 0-8027-0469-7)
   For those wanting a less erudite but still comprehensive history of musical instruments, this is a worthwhile sub-
stitute for the Marcuse book. It carries the history of musical instruments from their first known evolution and carefully
documents how each instrument influenced musical development.

MYSTICISM

Dictionary of Mysticism, ed. by Frank Gaynor. Citadel
Press, 1973. (ISBN 0-8065-0172-3)
   More than 2,200 terms are defined in the fields of
psychical research, spiritualism, alchemy, astrology, magic
and demonology. These are brief definitions but useful in
identification of various teachings and religions.

Christian Mysticism, by Harryl Haywood. Gordon Press.
(ISBN 0-87968-862-9)
   The history of Christian mysticism from St. John the
Revelator to the modern time.

NAMES, GEOGRAPHIC
see
GEOGRAPHY

NAMES, PERSONAL*

Black Names in America: Origins and Usage, ed. by Murray
   Heller. G. K. Hall, 1975. (ISBN 0-8161-1140-5)
      The origin, uses, history, and modifications of names
used by Blacks in America. The book is important for understanding the social significance of names in general and Black
names in particular. Black names have changed markedly
as their social position and self-esteem have improved.

The New Age Baby Name Book, by Sue Browder. Workman,
   1974. (ISBN 0-911104-31-3)
      The ever-present problem of what to name the baby
yields another book to help in the process. This one contains 3,000 names, from the most common to the very exotic,
from all parts of the world. For each name it gives the
source, the meaning and pronunciation of the name. In these
days of increasing desire for ethnic identification, this should
be a valuable aid in finding the right name. It even gives
astrological guides to the selection of names for those who
care for that sort of thing.

NATIONAL ANTHEMS

National Anthems of the World, by Martin Shaw, et al., eds.
   4th ed. rev. Pitman, 1975. (ISBN 0-273-00738-6)
      The information concerning the national anthems has
been supplied, in most cases, by the diplomatic embassies
and coordinated with printed sources. The result is a fairly
accurate presentation of the theme of the song even if there
is not a word-by-word translation. It is amazingly up to
date, including the words for new anthems adopted during
1975.

NATURAL RESOURCES*

State Administrative Officials Classified by Function. Council of State Governments, 1975. (ISBN 0-87292-013-5)
      This is a supplement to the Book of the States men-
tioned in Where to Find What. Under the heading NATURAL

RESOURCES you will find a listing of agencies and officials in each state.

Water Encyclopedia, ed. by David Keith Todd. Water Information Center, 1970. (ISBN 0-912394-01-3)
      This is a practical reference volume containing a
variety of water resources data, facts and statistics. It is
divided into nine chapters; climate and precipitation, hydrologic elements, surface water, ground water, water use,
water and pollution control, water quality, water resources
management, agencies and organizations, and constants and
conversion factors. Each chapter is a wealth of statistical
information in tabular form.

Water Resources of the World: Selected Statistics, ed. by
   Fritz van der Leeden. Water Information Center, 1975.
   (ISBN 0-912394-14-5)
      The best single source of information concerning the
water resources of the world. It has information on the
stream flow, water demand, quality of the water, and other
pertinent data for various countries of the world. It is
greatly strengthened by an excellent index and a clear indication of the source from which each bit of information was
selected.

NEWSPAPERMEN
see
JOURNALISTS

OCEANS

Atlas of the Sea, by Robert Barton. John Day, 1974.
   (ISBN 0-381-98267-X)
      Although this is called an atlas of the sea, it is much
more than that. The main position of the book is devoted to
the commercial aspects of the sea and what lies below, including not only the mineral resources, petroleum, etc. but also
the fish life and its potential for human food sources. Emphasis is also placed on the dangers of pollution to the sea
and its inhabitants. However, the book does give good maps
and descriptions of the basic current patterns and the phys-
iography of the sea bottom. It is a good introduction to the

study of oceanography, with excellent illustrations and easily
understood maps. As a result it can be of value to any
library serving a high school or older clientele.

OPERA*

The Encyclopedia of Opera, ed. by Leslie Orrey and Gilbert
    Chase. Scribner, 1976. (ISBN 0-684-13630-9)
    Despite the similarity of title to the Ewen book, this
is a definitely superior contribution. It is the most up-to-
date book on the subject and includes not only classic opera
but musical comedy as well. It is surprisingly well illustrated.

OPPOSITE MEANING
see
REVERSE DICTIONARY

PAINT AND PAINTING

Painting and Decorating Encyclopedia, ed. by William Brush-
    well. Goodheart, 1973. (ISBN 0-87006-160-7)
    This manual incorporates the fundamental principles
of painting and decorating with details concerning new paints,
materials and brushes, as well as an outline of color, color
mixing and styling.

PALMISTRY

        There are literally hundreds of cheap books purporting
to teach the art of reading palms. The two mentioned below
seem to be a cut above the others in presentation and ease
of explanation.

The Complete Encyclopedia of Practical Palmistry, by Marcel
    Broekman. Prentice-Hall, 1972. (ISBN 0-13-159988-7)

Your Past, Your Present and Your Future Through the Art
of Hand Analysis, by Mir Bashir. Doubleday, 1974.
(ISBN 0-385-02632-3)

PAPER

Commodity Yearbook, ed. by Harry Jiler. Commodity Research Bureau, Inc. Annual since 1939.
This publication gives price and production statistics
for each of the various commodities needed for our national
welfare. Under PAPER one finds statistics on the paper
industry of the United States. There are also statistics on
U. S. production and foreign trade of pulp wood.

Paper Yearbook. Ojibway Press. Annual.
This is the official source of current statistics concerning the manufacture of paper and paper products.

PARKS - NATIONAL

Exploring Our National Parks and Monuments, by Devereux
Butcher. 6th ed. rev. Houghton Mifflin, 1969.
(ISBN 0-395-07473-8)
A well illustrated introduction to our natural parks
and monuments. There are 354 photographs, many in color,
combined with excellent descriptions. This is a good introduction to America's parks.

National Parks and Landmarks. U. S. National Park Service.
Government Printing Office. Annual since 1949. (I29. 66)
This is a geographical listing by areas of the country
and then alphabetically by name of the park, historical site
or area. For each one it gives the name, the location, the
size and the outstanding features. It is well indexed and
should be received regularly by most libraries.

Guide to the National Parks: Their Landscape Geology, by
William H. Matthews. 2 vols. American Museum of
Natural History, 1968. (ISBN 0-385-08672-5)
Volume one is Western Parks and volume two is
Eastern Parks. Each is a comprehensive description of the

parks of its area and contains not only maps and descriptions
of the parks but also illustrations and discussions of the geology of each.   It is user-oriented and therefore popular in
presentation, but it is of great value to the average visitor.

PARKS - STATE

There are two good sources of information readily
available concerning State Parks and Recreation areas.   One
is the American Guide series book on the state desired (see
Where to Find What for complete listing).   The other source
of information is actually the best because it is continually
brought up to date.   I refer, of course, to the publications
of the State Recreation and Tourism Department.   They will
send, free of charge, the latest information on all aspects of
state tourism.   To find a complete listing of state agencies
in the field, see:

State Administrative Officials Classified by Function.   Coun-
    cil of State Governments, 1975.   (ISBN 0-87292-013-5)
        This is a supplement to the Book of the States.   Check
under headings TOURISM and PARKS.

PENSIONS
see
RETIREMENT

PERIODICALS - INDICES

Access, The Supplementary Index to Periodicals.   Gaylord.
    Three times a year since January 1975.
        This is intended as a supplement to Readers' Guide
and drops from indexing any periodical which is picked up
by that publication.   Currently 130-plus periodicals are indexed and it covers many taken by libraries but not indexed
elsewhere; for example, Playboy.

PERSONAL FINANCES*

Sylvia Porter's Money Book: How To Earn It, Spend It, Save
It, Invest It, Borrow It, and How to Use It to Better
Your Life, by Sylvia Porter. Doubleday, 1975. (ISBN
0-385-08484-6)
It is seldom that the writer gets as enthusiastic about
a book as I am about this one. It may not be the best book
for a library but it is one that I think every young person
should receive for a graduation present. It presents, in
easily read and, what is more important, easily applied
language, the principle of good home money management.
Buy it for yourself if not for your library.

PHARMACY

The National Formulary, compiled by American Pharmaceuti-
cal Association. Mack Publishing Company. Published
every 5 years since 1888.
This is an official publication of the American Pharma-
ceutical Association and gives reference standards and formu-
lation procedures for basic drugs, with official specifications
for their use.

New Handbook of Prescription Drugs, Official Names, Prices
and Sources for Patient and Doctor, by Richard Burack.
Rev. ed. Pantheon Books, 1967. (ISBN 0-394-42770-X)
"A handbook that lists the generic and brand names
for many drugs, pointing out that the consumers who buy
brand names pay more for the same drugs."

Pharmacopoeia of the United States of America. Mack Publishing Company. Published every five years since
1820.
This is the standard description of drugs and prepara-
tions recognized by the American Medical Association.

PHILANTHROPY

Fund Raising Techniques, by E. Hereward. Beekman, 1969.
(ISBN 0-220-79865-6)

The problems of fund raising are discussed with an emphasis on public relations and the public interest of the donors.

Philanthropic Giving, by F. Emerson Andrews. Russell
      Sage, 1950.
      A study of the foundations and funds which have con-
tributed so much to American life. It analyzes the many
types and grants available.

PHYSICS
see also
TECHNICAL TERMS

Dictionary of Scientific Biography, ed. by Charles Coulston
      Gillespie. Scribner, 1970- .
      This massive work is still in the process of publication
but the first 13 volumes are complete and are an excellent
addition both to biography and to scientific understanding.
The work is being prepared and published under the auspices
of the American Council of Learned Societies and when completed will be to the world of Science what the Dictionary
of American Biography is to the history of the United States.
The biographies place primary emphasis on the careers and
scientific achievements of the biographees, although personal
biographical data are included. This is probably too detailed
for the small library but any academic or public library
would benefit from its addition to the collection.

Encyclopedia of Physics, edited by Robert M. Besancon.
      2nd ed. Van Nostrand Reinhold, 1974. (ISBN 0-442-
      20691-7)
      This comprehensive encyclopedia attempts to include
articles aimed at all levels of comprehension from the very
beginner in the physical sciences up to the person with fairly
strong background in the field. It is written by numerous
contributors, each of whom is a recognized authority, and
each article progresses from a simple presentation of the
subject to more detailed and technical aspects, with references for further study and sometimes even suggestions for
experimentation.

McGraw-Hill Encyclopedia of Science and Technology, edited
      by Daniel N. Lapedes. 3rd ed. McGraw-Hill, 1971.
      (ISBN 0-07-079798-6)

This fifteen-volume encyclopedia is intended to be a concise but comprehensive work presenting pertinent information on every area of modern science and technology. It is written by 2,500 scientists and engineers, each a specialist in the field in which he writes. There are more than 7,600 articles written in such a manner as to give even the least acquainted reader the basic concepts of a science or technical idea. The length of the articles varies according to the complexity of the subject, but most are easily understood and many are accompanied by illustrations. This is a set which probably should be in all but the very smallest library.

PIRATES

Pirates in History, by Ralph T. Ward. York Press, 1974. (ISBN 0-912752-04-1)
The coming of the steam-powered ships spelled the end of a long and bloody history of piracy on the high seas. This book tells that history well and interestingly, including the stories of the individual pirates as well as famous victims. More importantly, it deals with the effect that pirates and piracy had on the development of naval warfare, ship design and maritime trade. It tells the story from the earliest pirates in the Mediterranean through to the final chapter.

PLACE NAMES
see
GEOGRAPHY

PLANTS*

Field Guide to Edible Wild Plants, by Bradford Angier. Stackpole, 1974. (ISBN 0-8117-0616-8)
Alphabetically arranged guide books have some built-in problems but this one should prove of interest to any library serving outdoors people or campers. For each entry a full description and color pictures are given.

A Guide to Medicinal Plants of the United States, by Arnold
and Connie Krochmal. Quadrangle, 1973. (ISBN 0-8129-
0261-0)
As I have repeated in every medical reference, the
library is not a medical center and should not dispense medical advice; therefore, I am happy that this book states quite
bluntly, "Self medication with Wild Plants is risky." If this
warning is heeded, this is an interesting book; 272 plants are
discussed, giving for each its common name, botanical name,
where it grows and which parts are to be used in medical
treatment.

PLAYING CARDS

History of Playing Cards and A Bibliography of Cards and
Gaming, by Catherine P. Hargrave. Peter Smith.
(ISBN 0-8446-2205-2)
This is a reprint of the only scholarly work I know
on the history of playing cards. It follows the development
of gaming cards by analyzing the collection of the United
States Playing Card Company.

POETRY
see
LITERATURE

POLICE*
see also
LAW ENFORCEMENT

Police Systems in the United States, ed. by Bruce Smith,
Jr. 2nd rev. ed. Harper and Row, 1960. (ISBN 0-06-
036090-9)
This outlines the various state, county and local police
systems and is a practical outline of police activities in the
country. It was compiled by interviews with police officials
and the study of police reports.

Municipal Yearbook. International City Managers. Annual

since 1934.

This is an authoritative résumé of activities and statistical data about all American cities. The information is
presented in two ways: signed articles dealing with local
developments in each field of municipal concern, i.e., taxes,
fire, police, etc., followed by statistical tables giving information on individual cities. There is a directory of all
major municipal employees for each city and a good bibliography on municipal problems.

POLITICAL PARTIES*

History of U.S. Political Parties, 1789-1972, ed. by Arthur
M. Schlesinger. 4 vols. Bowker, 1973. (ISBN 0-8352-
0594-0)

This is destined to be the major work on the history
of political parties in our country for some time to come.
It is arranged chronologically but each development is written
about by a person who has specialized in that particular aspect of American history.

National Party Conventions, 1831-1972. Congressional Quarterly, 1976. (ISBN 0-87187-093-2)

This book can be recommended for purchase by all
libraries. Its most important contribution is a "Chronology
of Nominating Conventions" which lists the nominees, gives
a picture where possible, and lists important events.

POLITICS

The American Political Dictionary, by Jack C. Plano and
Milton Greenberg. 4th edition. Holt, Rinehart and
Winston, 1976. (ISBN 0-03-016736-1)

This is the fourth edition of what is recognized as
the outstanding dictionary of political terms in our country.
It also has a subject arrangement which gives a summary of
concepts and court cases. Most academic and school libraries will find this helpful.

Guide to U.S. Elections, 1789-1974, compiled by Congressional Quarterly. Congressional Quarterly, 1974. (ISBN
0-87187-072-X)

Possibly the most comprehensive and complete book dealing with American elections on all levels of government ever published. It has the state-by-state popular vote for every presidential election since 1824. It has popular votes for every gubernatorial election since 1824 and House election returns since 1824. It has the popular vote for every Senator since the constitution was amended to require direct election of Senators. Good indexes.

POLLUTION

AIR

Handbook of Air Pollution, by James P. Sheehy, et al. U.S. Health Service. Government Printing Office, 1968. (FS 2.300:Ap44)
The introduction to this work states that it is intended "to consolidate the applicable portions of numerous references concerning the characteristics and behavior of air, gases and particles, and the chemistry of atmospheric pollutants and data of a general nature such as mathematics and common conversion factors."

Environmental Engineers Handbook. Volume Two: Air Pollution, ed. by Bela G. Liptak. Chilton, 1974. (ISBN 0-8019-5693-5)
This is part of a three-volume handbook, each volume concentrating on a specific aspect of environmental pollution. Volume II deals with air pollution and has chapters covering almost every phase of the problem and possible means of bettering or eliminating those problems. There is a glossary of basic terms and an excellent index.

LAND

Environmental Engineers Handbook. Volume III: Land Pollution, ed. by Bela G. Liptak. Chilton, 1974. (ISBN 0-8019-5694-3)
This volume covers the problems of land pollution and has chapters covering almost every aspect of the question and a discussion of possible means of bettering or eliminating those problems. There is a glossary and an excellent index.

WATER

Environmental Engineers Handbook. Volume I: Water Pol-
    lution, ed. by Bela G. Liptak. Chilton, 1974. (ISBN
    0-8019-5692-7)
        This volume covers water pollution and has chapters
concerning almost every aspect of the question and a discussion of possible means of bettering or eliminating those problems. There is a glossary and an excellent index.

PORTS*
see
CITIES

POSTAL SERVICES
see also
ZIP CODES

Directory of International Mail. U.S. Post Office Department.
    Government Printing Office. Annual.
        Contains detailed information about services, restric-
tions and costs of mail to other countries. The listing is
alphabetical by country.

Directory of Post Offices. U.S. Post Office Department.
    Government Printing Office. Annual.
        A listing of all Federal Post Offices along with Zip
Codes. The arrangement is alphabetical by states and then
by post office. It contains military as well as civilian post
offices.

POWER TOOLS

The Complete Handbook of Power Tools, by George R.
    Drake. Prentice-Hall, 1975.
        This is intended as an introduction to power tools to
be used by the amateur and is excellent for its coverage of
step-by-step procedures as well as standard safety procedures. For each tool described there are discussions of the

parts, means of operating and maintenance, as well as hints as to the kind of job for which the tool was intended. Unfortunately, the book is not "a complete handbook." It covers only stationary power tools and there are many portable hand-tools in use today.

PRESIDENTS - U.S. *

Burke's Presidential Families of the United States of America. Burke (distributed by Arco), 1975. (ISBN 0-85011-017-3)
Burke's Peerage comes to America--or so it seems. At any rate, the company so long famous for delineating the British Royalty turns its attention to the presidents of the United States and for each one traces his ancestry as far back as is possible. As might be expected, there is a special table listing American presidents with Royal blood. There is no book exactly like this on the market today; if you can afford it, buy it.

Presidential Portraits, by Virginia C. Purdy and Daniel J. Reed. National Collection of Fine Arts. Government Printing Office, 1968. (SI 11.2:P92)
There is a brief biographical sketch of each president and a photograph of his portrait. For each portrait it gives the size, the artist, the year painted in what medium it was done, and where it is currently located.

PRINTERS' MARKS

The Book: The Story of Printing and Bookmaking, ed. by Douglas C. McMurtrie. Oxford, 1943. (ISBN 0-19-50011-0)
This is the most popular and most easily read book in print on the history of printing and bookmaking. The first part is historical, beginning with the development of the alphabet and writing and then a discussion of early books and their publishers. The later half tells how a book is made. Pages 289-303 include a good section on printers' marks.

PRISONS*

National Prison Directory and Supplement, by Mary L. Bundy
and Rebecca G. Whaley. Urban Information Interpreters,
1975, 1976.
    This arranges prisons by state and then by locale and
gives an indication of the goals and activities of each prison.
There is an index to activities and a discussion of items on
prison reform. The book presents organizational profiles of
490 prison reform groups in the United States.

PROBABILITY TABLES

CRC Standard Mathematical Tables, ed. by Samuel M. Selby.
23rd ed. C. R. C. Press, 1975. (ISBN 0-87819-622-6)
    This is the most complete set of mathematical tables
available. It is a must for any academic library and would
be useful to most libraries. Under the index notation,
Probability and Statistics, one finds 22 pages of tables and
discussion of probability.

PSYCHIATRY*

A Psychiatric Glossary: A Meaning of Terms Frequently
Used in Psychiatry, by the American Psychiatric Association, Committee on Public Information. 4th ed. Basic
Books, 1975. (ISBN 0-465-06467-1)
    Originally published in 1957, this has become the most
reliable of sources of psychiatry terms, but it is more than
a glossary. There are tables of psychological tests, schools
and approaches. This will prove of great help in answering
questions in the field of mental health.

PUBLIC HEALTH*

Directory and Index of Safety and Health Laws and Code,
ed. by Richard M. Bank and Thomas H. Seymour. U. S.
Bureau of Labor Standards. Government Printing Office,
1969. (L16. 2:Sa 1/31)

There is both a subject and a classified index to help one find the desired laws in any state of the country. This does not give the text of the laws but a legal citation to the proper code book of statutes or regulations.

PUBLISHERS

Books in Print. R. R. Bowker. Annual. 4 volumes.
The invaluable book which originally was meant as an index to Publishers' Trade List Annual is now an index to author and title entries for all books currently in print. Volume four (TITLES) has an appendix which lists almost every publisher in the United States and Canada. For each, it gives the address including zip code, the telephone number including area code, and the ISBN prefix for the company.

Literary Market Place; The Business Directory of American Book Publishing. R. R. Bowker Company. Annual since 1941.
This is not only a register of the personnel in the publishing fields but also a guide for persons wanting either to sell a particular type of writing or to locate a particular type of writing. It is arranged by Book Publishers, Authors' Agents, Writers' Associations, Employment Agencies, and finally by periodicals and reference books. There is an excellent index.

Writer's Market, ed. by Lynne Ellinwood. Writer's Digest. Annual since 1930.
This is undoubtedly the best source of information on markets for written materials. It lists the various markets available and gives the addresses of the companies, the names of the editors for each type of material, information concerning the rates of pay, the time of reporting and any special requirements needed for each magazine or company. The arrangement is by type of publication and by type of material desired, with a good index for finding the desired publication. This is a book that should be in any library which has questions from potential writers.

PUPPETRY

Expert Puppet Technique, by Eric Bramall and Christopher

C. Somerville. Plays, 1966. (ISBN 0-8238-0068-7)
This is a manual for production of puppet plays and contains information concerning script-writing, puppet making and set designing. It is an easily understood but fully reliable introduction to string puppetry.

Puppet Theatre Handbook, by Marjorie H. Batchelder. Harper & Row, 1947. (ISBN 0-06-000270-0)
This quite dated handbook in the field of puppetry still remains one of the very best sources for planning a puppet show. Instructions are given for costuming the puppet, making stages, stage lighting and staging special effects such as thunder.

Puppet Plays for Young Players, by Lewis Mahlmann and David C. Jones. Plays, 1974. (ISBN 0-8238-0152-7)
An excellent collection of puppet plays for use with elementary school children.

Art of the Puppet, by Bil Baird. Plays, 1966. (ISBN 0-8238-0067-9)
An introductory book by the current leader in the field of puppetry. It is a good history of puppet shows and puppetry as an art form. Excellent illustrations and a good index make this a worthwhile book.

QUOTATIONS *

The previous book referred to several books of quotations. The following are examples of collections of quotations from specific subject areas:

Concise Dictionary of Religious Quotations, compiled by William Neil. Eerdmans, 1974. (ISBN 0-8028-3451-5)
These quotations are drawn from many sources, both Christian and non-Christian. The prime source, as one would expect in a western country, is the Bible, but other sacred books are included as well as the writings of St. Augustine and others. It is well arranged and has an excellent index.

The Filmgoer's Book of Quotes, compiled by Leslie Halliwell. Arlington House, 1973. (ISBN 0-87000-285-6)
Maybe this is trivia but it is the trivia that many

people enjoy. It does lack something as a reference source because of its haphazard arrangement but there is an index to both the quotation and the quoter. Fun if not really valuable.

RADIO*
see
CITIZEN'S BAND RADIO

RAILROADS*

American Railroads, by John F. Stover. University of Chicago, 1961 (repr., 1976). (ISBN 0-226-77655-7)
This is a part of the "Chicago History of American Civilization" series and describes the growth of the railroads and how they affected every aspect of American life.

Rail Facts and Feats, ed. by John Marshall. Two Continents, 1974. (ISBN 0-8467-0005-0)
This is another outgrowth of the Guinness Book of World Records, doing for the railroad world what that book does on a general scale. It gives the highest, biggest, smallest, and longest records; in addition, there are mini-biographies of pioneers and leaders in the field of railroading. Because of the topical arrangement one has to use the index to find specific information.

REFRIGERATION

For books dealing with the air conditioning aspect of this subject see that heading in Where to Find What.

Refrigeration, Air Conditioning and Cold Storage, ed. by Raymond C. Gunther. 2nd rev. ed. Chilton, 1969. (ISBN 0-8019-5364-2)
This book covers all phases of refrigeration and cold storage and their many applications. It is particularly good as a "how-to" book and gives instructions on installation and maintenance of almost every type of equipment in the field.

RELIGIONS

Religions of America: Fermont and Faith in an Age of
  Crisis, ed. by Leo Rosten. Rev. ed. Simon & Schuster,
  1975. (ISBN 0-671-21970-7)
    This is the second edition of a book that has become
a recognized source for ready information on religion and religious sects in America. It has two sections. The first one
gives basic information about the 16 primary denominations
and the second part is a study of issues and the stand that
each church takes on each issue.

ATLAS

Historical Atlas of the Religions of the World, edited by I. R.
  Farugi and D. E. Sopher. Macmillan, 1974. (ISBN 0-
  02-336400-9)
    This covers over 20 world religions, showing where
each flourishes. Both dead and current religions are discussed and charted. Maps show the spread of each religion and
its extent at specific dates. There is a good bibliography and
an excellent index.

RESTAURANTS

    For anyone traveling in Europe the Michelin Guides
are absolute musts for restaurants and hotels.

The Michelin Green and Red Guides. French and European
  Publications.
    These two sets of books, originally published by the
Michelin Tire Company for the use of its customers, have
over the years become the authentic guide for travelers to
all parts of Europe. The Red Guides are published about
Easter of each year and present data on various cities and
towns of Europe, giving for each the population, principal
attractions and, most importantly, a listing of the major
hotels and restaurants, graded by type of service and official
government rating. The ratings given the hotels and restaurants are very accurate and highly prized by establishments
listed therein. Hotel rates and restaurant prices are also
given. The following Red Guides are available.

| France | Italy | Benelux |
| Germany | Paris | Spain & Portugal |

The Red Guides for Benelux and Spain also carry sightseeing information.

The Green Guides are not revised annually and are intended to point out places of interest and the most advantageous routes within each country in the time available. For each town, the following information is given   a brief historical note, the main tourist attractions (rated one, two or three stars depending upon importance), and a listing of other sights in the immediate area (also rated one, two or three stars).   There are many maps to important tourist areas and an estimate of how much time should be devoted to each area.   There are nineteen Green Guides to various sections of France and individual guides to the following locations:

| Austria | New York City | Germany |
| Portugal | Italy | Switzerland |

For travel in the United States, the area guides provided by the American Automobile Association to its members provide a similar but much less satisfactory service.

RETIREMENT*

The Retirement Handbook: A Complete Planning Guide to
Your Future, ed. by Henry Schmidt. 5th edition.
Barnes & Noble, 1973. (ISBN 0-06-463366-7)
This is the fifth edition of an immensely popular and helpful book which first appeared in 1953. It is written in a popular style and is easily read and understood. Some suggestions may be questionable but, in general, this is an excellent handbook for anyone planning retirement. It covers such aspects as Social Security and the ways to be sure that you receive all benefits, as well as a discussion of the Medicare and Medicaid programs. It also has sections on leisure time activities and investment planning for retirement. This last section, which could have been the most valuable, is not as well done as the rest of the book.

Handbook on Retirement Services for Army Personnel and
Their Families, by U.S. Department of the Army.
Government Printing Office, 1969. (D 101.22: 600- 5/3)
Although directed at retired army personnel, the
carry-over to other services is great and this book can
answer questions for all branches. It includes anticipated
financial benefits as well as other perquisites.

For a general discussion of pensions and retirement:

The Debate on Private Pensions. American Enterprise Institute, 1968.
This is one of the American Enterprise Institute's
"Legislative Analysis" series and is a thorough look at the
future. It covers such questions as funding, vesting, probability and reinsurance.

Digest of 100 Selected Pension Plans under Collective Bar-
gaining, by U.S. Department of Labor. Bulletin 1435.
Government Printing Office. (Basic manual and loose
leaf supplements) (L2.3 1435)
This publication of the Department of Labor is intended
to give the user an idea of the variety of pension plans that
are available to various types of workers or professions.
The information is presented in tabular form for each company and gives an excellent view of the pension systems of
industry.

For information concerning state retirement plans:

State Administrative Officials Classified by Function. Council
of State Governments, 1975. (ISBN 0-87292-013-5)
This is a special supplement to The Book of the
States. Under the heading of Retirement Systems you will
find the names and addresses of the officials and agencies
within each state that handle pensions and retirement benefits. Almost all states will send one copy of the current
regulations upon request.

REVERSE DICTIONARY

Bernstein's Reverse Dictionary, by Theodor M. Bernstein.
Quadrangle, 1975. (ISBN 0-8129-0566-0)
How often have you been puzzled by a question such
as "what is a sentence called that reads the same forward

or backward?" This book attempts to answer those questions by arranging key words from ordinary definitions alphabetically and then directing one to the desired word. In this case, under sentence, you would find "reads forward or backward" --palindrome.

ROCKS*
see also
MINERALS

Gems and Minerals of America: A Guide to Rock Collecting, by Jay E. Ransom. Harper, 1975. (ISBN 0-06-013512-3)

Jay Ransom is an expert on rock hunting and rock collection and in this book he has taken each state, and within the states each county, and listed the places where various types of rocks may be found. As important as this atlas-type information is, it is topped by his section called "Fundamentals of Rock Collecting." In this he has photographs of various rocks and minerals in color, and instructions on how to treat and store the stones one collects.

SAINTS*
see
SIGNS AND SYMBOLS

SCHOOLS

GENERAL

Patterson's American Education, ed. by Norman F. Elliott. Educational Directories. Published annually since 1904.

The subtitle adequately describes the purpose of this book: "Presenting information about State Departments of Education, public school systems and their superintendents, public high and junior high schools and their principals. Also private high schools, public and private colleges, universities, professional, vocational and preparatory schools. All arranged and classified alphabetically for easy reference."

PRIVATE

Handbook of Private Schools. An Annual Descriptive Study
     of Independent Education. Boston, Mass.: Porter Sar-
     gent. Annual since 1915.
     This is the best source of authoritative information
concerning the 2,000 boarding and day schools in this country.
For each school, the following information is given: name,
address, presiding officer and names of outstanding adminis-
trators of the school, cost, size of student body, faculty-
student ratio, physical facilities and age spans covered. In
addition to the strictly informational section, there is a section of paid advertisements called "Private Schools Illustrated"
which presents frankly promotional materials in an attractive
way.

PUBLIC

Educational Directory. U.S. Office of Education. Govern-
     ment Printing Office. Annual since 1894. (From 1894
     to 1911 as a chapter in annual report of U.S. Office of
     Education.)
     This is a comprehensive directory of all educational
institutions of the United States. It is published in four
parts: Part I, State Governments; Part II, Public School
Systems; Part III, Higher Education; Part IV, Educational
Associations. Part II lists every school district with more
than 300 students, except for those run by the states, the
federal government or as adjuncts to a college or university.
Arrangement is alphabetical, first by state and then by local
unit. Gives superintendent, his address, enrollment and
grades covered as well as administrative units in each district.

SUMMER

A Guide to Summer Camps and Summer Schools. Porter
     Sargent. Annual since 1946.
     This is the most comprehensive guide to summer
camps and schools available. Annual revision keeps the
information, even of such variable items as cost, fairly
accurate. It is arranged geographically and then by type of
camp or school. For each camp or school one finds the
camp name, the address, date of forming, director's name,
and a summary of the programs offered.

SCIENCE
see also
TECHNICAL TERMS

<u>McGraw-Hill Encyclopedia of Science and Technology</u>, 3rd ed.
edited by Daniel N. Lapedes. McGraw-Hill, 1971.
(ISBN 0-07-079798-6)
This fifteen-volume encyclopedia is intended to be a
concise but comprehensive work presenting pertinent information on every area of modern science and technology. It is
written by 2,500 scientists and engineers, each a specialist
in the field in which he writes. There are more than 7,600
articles written in such a manner as to convey to even the
least acquainted reader the basic concepts of a science or
technical idea. The length of the articles varies with the
complexity of the topic, but each is easily understood and
many are accompanied by illustrations. This is a set which
probably should be in all but the very smallest library.

<u>Dictionary of Scientific Biography</u>, edited by Charles Coulston
Gillespie. Charles Scribner's Sons, 1970- .
This massive work is still in the process of publication but the first 13 volumes are complete and are an excellent addition to both biography and scientific understanding.
The work is being prepared and published under the auspices
of the American Council of Learned Societies and when completed will be to the world of science what the <u>Dictionary of</u>
<u>American Biography</u> is to the history of the United States.
The biographies place primary emphasis on the careers and
scientific achievements of the biographees, although personal
biographical data are included. This is probably too detailed
for the small library but any academic or public library
would benefit from its addition to the collection.

SCIENCE - FICTION
see
BOOKS - PLOTS AND CHARACTERS

SEALS, STATE

<u>The Book of the States</u>. Published by the Council of State

Governments.   Biennial since 1935.
This is a comprehensive guide to state governments.
For each state there is a directory of officials, general information and statistics, and many articles dealing with the problems and recent developments of state governments in the past biennium.   There is an appendix giving pertinent facts such as state flowers, birds, etc.   There is also a depiction of the seal for each state.

American Symbols: The Seals and Flags of the Fifty States, by Henry Hatton.   Public Affairs Press, 1974.   (ISBN 0-8183-0128-7)
Describes not only the flags but the seals of the various states as well.   It also has a good description and history of the national flag and seal.

SEASHELLS
see
SHELLS

SERVICE ACADEMIES

The most common questions concerning the service academies are about the life of the cadets and the admission standards for entrance but there are often requests for listings of graduates.   Each type of question will be answered in this section.

ENTRANCE REQUIREMENTS

There are five service academies sponsored by the Federal Government for the training of officers in the various branches of the military and naval services of the United States.   For information concerning the requirements for admission and appointments, the best source is the Admissions Officer of the academy concerned; write and request a catalog and entrance information.   The persons to write to in each case are as follows:

U.S. Military Academy
Admissions Officer
U.S. Military Academy
West Point, N.Y.   10996

U. S. Naval Academy
    Dean of Admissions
    U. S. Naval Academy
    Annapolis, Maryland   21402

U. S. Air Force Academy
    Registrar
    U. S. Air Force Academy
    Colorado Springs, Colorado   80840

U. S. Coast Guard Academy
    Admissions Officer
    U. S. Coast Guard Academy
    New London, Connecticut   06320

U. S. Merchant Marine Academy
    Admissions Officer
    U. S. Merchant Marine Academy
    Kings Point, New York   11024

Additional information can be obtained from your
Congressman or Senator since the majority of assignments
are made upon recommendation of the elected officials.
Each one has his or her own standards for selection.

Most Senators or Congressmen use some type of
qualification testing to determine who will be appointed from
their districts, and there are several good introductions to
such tests. Although there is some question as to how much
help such books are in the actual taking of the tests, they
do introduce the student to the type of questions asked and
familiarize the applicant with the testing procedure. Each
book has sample tests and sample questions for study prior
to examination.

How to Qualify for the Service Academies, by Monro Mac-
    Closkey.   Richard Rosen Press, 1964.   (ISBN 0-8239-
    0138-6)

U. S. Service Academy Admission Tests.   Arco Press, 1966.
    (ISBN 0-688-01544-6)

LIFE OF THE CADET

Luckily, questions of this nature usually come from
boys and girls in grade school or high school who are considering entering one of the academies, because the only
really good books on the subject are aimed at that age level.

For grade school readers:

West Point: Cadets, Training and Equipment, by C. B.
   Colby. Coward Press, 1963. (ISBN 0-698-30392-X)

Air Force Academy: Cadets, Training and Equipment, by
   C. B. Colby. Coward Press, 1962. (ISBN 0-698-30005-
   X)

Coast Guard Academy: Cadets, Training and Equipment, by
   C. B. Colby. Coward Press, 1965. (ISBN 0-698-30449-
   7)

Annapolis: Cadets, Training and Equipment, by C. B. Colby.
   Coward Press, 1964. (ISBN 0-698-30014-9)

For high school students:

Annapolis: The Life of a Midshipman, by Jack Engeman.
   Rev. ed. Lothrop, 1965. (ISBN 0-688-41596-2)

U.S. Air Force Academy: The Life of a Cadet, by Jack
   Engeman. Lothrop, 1961. (ISBN 0-688-41597-0)

West Point: The Life of a Cadet, by Jack Engeman. Rev.
   ed. Lothrop, 1967. (ISBN 0-688-41598-9)

Both of these series are excellent introductions to the
life of the student at the service academy. As the dates
indicate, they are seriously in need of revision to cover the
admission of girls to the schools as well as other advances,
but they are the best currently available.

GRADUATES

For questions about officers who have graduated from
one of the academies, there is a fairly simple solution; just
consult the annual register of graduates of the various academies. These publications not only list by class rank every
graduate of the academy, but also give for each a brief biographical account of his military service including major
assignments, dates of promotions, any medals or honors received, date of retirement and present address.

Register of Graduates and Former Cadets of the U.S. Military
   Academy. West Point Alumni Foundation, Inc. Annual.

Register of Alumni, Graduates, and Former Naval Cadets
and Midshipmen. U. S. Naval Academy, Alumni Association. Annual.

Register of Graduates of the U. S. Air Force Academy. U. S.
Air Force Academy, Association of Graduates. Annual.

SEWAGE DISPOSAL

Municipal Yearbook. International City Managers. Annual
since 1934.
This is an authoritative résumé of activities and statistical data about all American cities. The information is
presented in two ways: signed articles dealing with local
developments in each field of municipal concern, i. e., taxes,
fire, police, etc., followed by statistical tables giving information on individual cities. There is a directory of all major
municipal employees for each city and a good bibliography
on municipal problems. Each annual volume will have a
chapter dealing with sewage disposal problems under the
headings SANITATION and WATER SYSTEMS.

Sewage Treatment, by Karl Imhoff and Gordon Fair. 2nd
ed. Wiley, 1956. (ISBN 0-471-42669-5)
This quite basic book gives useful and trustworthy
information on all types of sewage treatment and plants.

SHAKESPEARE*

The New Century Shakespeare Handbook, edited by Sandra
Clark and T. H. Long. Prentice-Hall, 1974. (ISBN
0-13-612093-8)
Wherever there are questions about Shakespeare or
his works, particularly in the high school or college library,
this book will prove helpful. It is divided into five sections:
a biography, an analysis of the theater of Shakespeare's time
including play production, a discussion of his major poetical
works, a bibliography of works dealing with Shakespeare published since 1945 and, possibly the most usable part, an
alphabetical dictionary of play titles complete with plots and
characters. The title entries give not only the general plot

but also the historical source of the play as well as listing
important characters in each play and discussing the general
characteristics of each.

SHELLS*

American Seashells, ed. by R. Tucker Abbott.   2nd ed.
    Van Nostrand Reinhold, 1974.   (ISBN 0-442-20228-8)
        This is intended for the serious student who has spent
enough time in the field to have mastered the biological terminology involved.   It is an expensive item but for answering
questions concerning seashells and mollusks, it is an invaluable addition to the collection.   There are full descriptions of more than 2000 species and listings of even more.
It covers shells found from Northern Mexico through Canada.
The excellent text is supplemented by 4000 photographs and
drawings as well as 24 full-color plates.   An index is given
to both scientific and common names.

Collecting World Seashells, by Alan Major.   Arco, 1974.
    (ISBN 0-668-03387-8)
        This one is intended for the novice: it includes intro-
ductory material on techniques of collecting and preserving
specimens.   The major portion of the book, though, is devoted to simple descriptions of the shells of the world.   This
is a collector's guide and therefore is devoted to the shell
itself, not the animal found therein.

The Collector's Encyclopedia of Shells, by Peter S. Dance.
    McGraw-Hill, 1974.   (ISBN 0-07-015290-X)
        This is a beautiful and useful book for shell identifica-
tion.   There are careful descriptions of over 2000 shells
and more than 1500 color photographs, pictures and descriptions are inter-related to make identification relatively easy.
This one can be used by both the novice and the expert.

SHIPS*
see also
SUBMARINES

Battleships: United States Battleships in World War II, by

William H. Garzke and Robert O. Dulin. Naval Institute
    Press, 1976. (ISBN 0-87021-099-8)
    This is the definitive technical history of all battle-
ships designed and constructed since 1930. It covers not only
their design and construction but also gives a summary of
the operational history of each ship. There are excellent
line drawings of all principal technical points such as deck
plans, armor profile and armament as well as a good discussion of the background of each development. For any
library whose clientele is interested in naval armament, this
book is a must.

Merchant Ships of the World in Color, 1910-1929, by Lau-
    rence Dunn. Macmillan, 1975. (ISBN 0-02-53392)
    This is the first of what promises to be an excellent
series of books dealing with the history and identification of
merchant vessels. It covers all facets of the field from
tramp steamers to ocean liners, including freighters and
tankers as well. In this volume there are 80 color plates
illustrating more than 100 different vessels, along with a
history and specifications for each. When the series is
completed it will be a worthy companion to the Jane's books.

SIGNS AND SYMBOLS*

Symbol Sourcebook: An Authoritative Guide to International
    Graphic Symbols, ed. by Henry Dreyfuss and R. Buck-
    minster Fuller. McGraw-Hill, 1972. (ISBN 0-07-017837-
    2)
    A well-illustrated guide to symbols and signs used in
the field of international trade.

American Symbols: The Seals and Flags of the Fifty States,
    by Henry Hatton. Public Affairs Press, 1974. (ISBN
    0-8183-0128-7)
    This book corrects the one fatal weakness in the
Smith book (below). It describes not only the flags but the
seals of the various states as well. It also has a good description and history of the national flag and seal.

Flags Through the Ages and Across the World, by Whitney
    Smith. McGraw-Hill, 1975. (ISBN 0-07-059093-1)
    This is a definitive history of world flags from most
ancient days to those now waving over the United Nations

Plaza. It illustrates in full color and describes in vivid
language the flags of the world. Although it is primarily on
national standards, it also includes flags of international
organizations such as SEATO, NATO, OAS and others. It
is also useful because it has a well-illustrated section devoted
to animals and symbols used in heraldry as well as in sports
and industry. The book's one major weakness is that it does
not cover the flags of the individual states of the United States.
In other respects it is possibly the best book available on
flags, symbols, etc. and I would recommend it for inclusion
in every library.

RELIGION

How to Distinguish the Saints in Art by Their Costumes,
    Symbols and Attributes, by Arthur de Bles. Gale Pub-
    lishing, 1975 (reprint of 1925 ed.). (ISBN 0-8103-4125-
    5)
        Good for symbolic costumes and forms associated with
the Saints of the Christian faith.

Handbook of Symbols in Christian Art, by Gertrude Grace
    Sill. Macmillan, 1975. (ISBN 0-02-000850-3)
        This is a dictionary arrangement of symbolic cate-
gories such as flowers, animals, clothing. For each symbol,
its history is traced to earliest known use, often in the
Bible itself.

SOCIAL SCIENCES

Social Science Research Handbook, by Raymond G. McInnis
    and James W. Scott. Barnes and Noble, 1975. (ISBN
    0-06-460140-4)
        This is a bibliographical guide to almost all the ref-
erence sources in the field of the Social Sciences. It could
easily be used as a buying guide for a beginning collection
in the field and will probably be used in just that way by
many colleges and schools.

SOLAR ENERGY
see also
ENERGY

Solar Directory, ed. by Carolyn Pesko. New ed. Ann
    Arbor Science Publications, 1975. (ISBN 0-250-40109-6)
    This is primarily a directory of the manufacturers,
distributors and individuals concerned with the production of
solar energy but it is also helpful because of the descriptions of various methods used to cool or heat homes and
other buildings in the United States. There is an extensive
annotated bibliography and a list of information services available to anyone interested in the subject.

SPACE

History of Rocketry and Space Travel, by Wernher Von
    Braun and Frederick L. Ordway III. Rev. ed. T. Y.
    Crowell, 1975. (ISBN 0-690-00588-1)
    Written by the pioneer in modern rocketry, this is an
excellent introduction to the history of man's search for the
stars, covering from the earliest efforts to the present day.

New Illustrated Space Encyclopedia, by Erik Bergaust. Rev.
    ed. Putnam, 1970. (ISBN 0-399-60487-1)
    Although intended for the school-age audience, this is
a worthwhile introductory book for anyone interested in space
travel. There are definitions of almost 3000 space and as-
tronautical terms as well as biographies of outstanding figures
in the space program.

SPIDERS

The Spider Book, by John H. Comstock. Rev. ed. Com-
    stock, 1948. (ISBN 0-8014-0084-8)
    An excellent source book for information on and iden-
tification of the spiders, scorpions and other similar species
found in the United States and Canada. There is an analytical
key to their classifications and habits.

SPORTS*
see also
GAMES

Oxford Companion to World Sports and Games, ed. by John
 Arlott.   Oxford, 1975.   (ISBN 0-19-211538-3)
  This is similar in approach to the other books in the
Oxford Companion series.   An excellent book of reference,
it is intended as an introduction to all sports and games
played on the international scene and will be of help to anyone trying to understand a sport, even the first time that he
or she sees it.   There are easily understood descriptive passages describing how each sport is played and scored, as
well as historical and biographical sections dealing with sports
history and personalities.   The arrangement is alphabetical
and the entries, though generally short, provide an excellent
introduction to each sport or game.   It is a book that should
be in just about any library.

Rules of the Game, by The Diagram Group.   Two Continents
 Publ., 1974.   (ISBN 0-8467-0025-5)
  This is an illustrated and diagrammed book explaining
the playing rules of most of the world's sports.   There is a
detailed list of rules as well as diagrams showing the layout
and measurements of the playing fields.

Sports Book: An Unabashed Assembly of Heroes, Strategies,
 Records and Events, edited by Min S. Yee and Don K.
 Wright.   Holt Rinehart & Winston, 1975.   (ISBN 0-03-
 015101-5)
  Another book that can be highly recommended for any
library which has to deal with sports inquiries.   In this
book, 30 sports are assembled along with anecdotes of outstanding players and important games or events in history.
One interesting feature not easily located elsewhere is a listing of all athletes currently making more than $100,000 per
year.

Sports Quiz Book, by Mary Albert and Stan Fischler.
 Grosset, 1975.

Football Quizbook, by Al Goldberg.   Drake, 1975.   (ISBN
 0-8473-1105-8)
  These two books, although issued by different publishers, are similar in approach and coverage.   The first is,
of course, more comprehensive than the second since it
covers all sports, but each is excellent for background on
sports and athletes as well as for answers to many different
types of sports trivia.   Neither would really classify as a
reference book but they will be a real help to the librarian
who has many sport enthusiasts as users.

SUBMARINES

It seems a little picky to list submarines separately rather than under ships, but the Navy refers to them as boats and I would not want to argue with the Navy.

The Illustrated History of the Submarine, by Edward Horton.
Doubleday, 1974. (ISBN 0-385-05614-1)
This book covers the history of the submarine and submarine warfare from the very first endeavor by Cornelius Drebbel in Holland in the early 17th century right down to the modern atomic submarines. The textual history is supplemented by photos, or by paintings and diagrams when a photo is not available, which show the development of the submarine. Since submarines reached their full military capabilities only in World Wars I and II, there are chapters which deal specifically with each of those wars.

SUMMER CAMPS

A Guide to Summer Camps and Summer Schools. Porter
Sargent. Annual since 1946.
This is the most comprehensive guide to summer camps and schools available. Annual revision keeps the information, even of such variable items as cost, fairly accurate. It is arranged geographically and then by type of camp or school. For each camp or school, one finds the camp name, the address, the date of forming, the director's name, and a summary of the programs offered.

TARIFFS

Tariff Schedules of the United States, Annotated. U.S.
Tariff Commission. Government Printing Office. Published irregularly.
This is the latest compilation of the legal bases for tariffs and tariff schedules, with annotations explaining changes and applications.

United States Import Duties. U.S. Tariff Commission. Government Printing Office. Published irregularly.

A simple listing of duties arranged by categories.

Custom House Guide. Budd Publications. Annual.
This is a non-governmental publication which gives miscellaneous information concerning all aspects of the import/export trade. It is worldwide in scope.

TECHNICAL TERMS

McGraw-Hill Dictionary of Scientific and Technical Terms, ed. by Daniel N. Lapedes. McGraw-Hill, 1974. (ISBN 0-07-045257-1)
This dictionary identifies and gives clear definitions of the many technical and scientific terms in use today. The length of the definition varies with the complexity of the subject. Illustrations accompany some definitions for greater clarification. This is a "must" for almost any library. Its weakness, if it can be said to have one, is that it does not adequately give pronunciation or syllabification, but concentrates on meaning of words.

TELESCOPES
see also
ASTRONOMY

Standard Handbook for Telescope Making, by Neale E. Howard. Crowell, 1959. (ISBN 0-690-76784-6)
This is a practical guide for the beginner or amateur astronomer and gives easily understood and followed instructions for making your own telescope. It explains the processes of grinding, mounting and adjusting the telescope.

TEXTILES

Encyclopedia of Textiles. American Fabrics Magazine. Textile Books. 1960. (ISBN 0-87245-507-6)
This basic reference work on the textile industry covers the history and origin or man-made fibers and cotton

cloth, silk, spinning, weaving and the printing of textiles.
It has an excellent glossary of textile terms.

Modern Textile and Apparel Dictionary, ed. by George E.
    Linton. 4th rev. ed. Textile Book Service, 1973.
    (ISBN 0-87245-500-9)
        Originally called the Modern Textile Dictionary, this
edition has been further expanded in defining terms, phrases
and words used in textile and clothing production. It is especially good for products, chemical construction and man-
made fibers. More than 16,000 terms are included in this
prime source.

Textile Handbook. American Home Economic Association.
    5th ed. The Association, 1974. (ISBN 0-8461-1611-1)
        This answers most of the more common questions
concerning fabric safety, trademarks and legal aspects. It
gives a good summary of the latest trends and developments
as well as charts and tables giving information on trade
marks, hints on care, etc. There is an excellent bibliography as well as statistical tables.

THERMOMETERS

Science for the Citizen, by Lancelot Hogben. 4th ed. Nor-
    ton, 1957. (ISBN 0-393-06324-0)
        This encyclopedic volume is intended as a self-educa-
tion guide for the interested laymen in all fields of science.
It covers aspects of chemistry, physics, biology and psychol-
ogy. While popular in treatment, it is quite accurate in
presentation. There is a good discussion of the history and
development of the thermometer and its various types.

TIMETABLES

        In this day of the WATS-line telephone and free 800
numbers offered by many companies, it seems an effort in
futility to keep timetables in the library but you often get
asked for them and each transportation industry issues them.
Most airlines will send your library current schedules if you
ask for them. The following are general timetables.

Official Airline Guide.   American Aviation Publications.
Published monthly.

Russell's Official National Motor Coach Guide.   Russell's
Guides, Inc.   Published monthly.

Official Guide of the Railways and Steam Navigation Lines
of the U.S., Canada, Mexico and Cuba.   National Rail-
way Publication Co.   Published monthly.

Official Steamship Guide: International.   Transportation
Guides, Inc.   Published monthly with various titles.

TRADEMARKS*

Consumer's Sourcebook: A Directory and Guide to Government Organizations, Associations, Centers and Institutes,
Media Services, Company and Trademark Information and
Bibliographical Materials Leading to Consumer Topics,
Sources of Recourse and Advisory Information, ed. by
Paul Wasserman and Jean Morgan.   Gale, 1974.   (ISBN
0-8103-0381-7)
With a subtitle like that one, there is no need for an
annotation.   This is an excellent sourcebook for such information as telephone numbers and addresses as well as the names
of important personnel to contact when lodging complaints or
requesting information.   Also useful for tradenames and trademarks.

Textile Handbook.   American Home Economic Association.
5th ed.   The Association, 1974.   (ISBN 0-8461-1611-1)
This answers most of the more common questions
concerning fabric safety, trademarks and legal aspects.   It
gives a good summary of the latest trends and fabric developments as well as charts and tables giving information on
trademarks, hints on care, etc.   There is an excellent bibliography and statistical tables.

TRAVEL*

Selected Guide to Travel Books, ed. by Susan Nueckel.

Fleet Press, 1974. (ISBN 0-8303-0131-3)
  Although Where to Find What has a good listing of preliminary travel guide books, this excellent bibliography offers many additional titles in the field of travel. It is arranged by type of travel and by location, with an index to subjects. For each title listed it gives a very brief annotation and the usual order information. In this first edition some very good guidebook series, such as Fodor, are not listed but the book does give a good broad view of the subject.

World Travelers' Almanac, ed. by Bill Munster. Rand
    McNally, 1975. (ISBN 0-528-84080-0)
  This differs from the usual travel book in that it is not a guide to information about places to visit but a guide to how to plan and how to travel. It includes an annotated list of 1000 travel books and gives addresses of tour operators and national tourist information offices. It is an excellent book.

TRIVIA
see also
FACTS

The Trivia Encyclopedia, by Fred L. Worth. Brooke House,
    1974. (ISBN 0-912588-12-8)
  This is an alphabetical arrangement of all sorts of miscellaneous information. It answers such questions as the Lone Ranger's real name, the date of the first Olympic Games, etc. Very enjoyable to browse in but sometimes frustrating if your thought processes don't match the compiler's.

The Trivia Quizbook, by Gilbert W. Davies. Drake Pub-
    lishers, 1975. (ISBN 0-8473-1108-2)
  This is similar to the above title but is in the form of 52 quizzes with answers in the back. Once again, fun to browse, but it's very frustrating trying to find a specific item.

TROPICAL FISH*

Guide to Aquarium Fishes, by Klaus Paysan. Quadrangle

Press, 1975. (ISBN 0-8129-0564-4)
    While this book adds little to the book collection that cannot be found elsewhere, its arrangement and illustrations make it worth considering. It is designed to provide easy identification and for each aquarium fish it gives shape, colors, and basic information concerning its care and feeding. More than 500 species are introduced and each has a key based on the shape of the fish. There are color photographs of almost every variety. The descriptive passages are brief but easily understood.

The Dell Encyclopedia of Tropical Fish, by T. W. Julian. Delacorte, 1974. (ISBN 0-440-01765-3)
    This small book lists only about 400 varieties of tropical fish. It is intended for the beginner or the home aquariumist. More than 200 full-color illustrations of various species are accompanied by easily understood information concerning the various ailments which may attack your fish, the proper foods for each variety and the proper use of plants and other objects in your aquarium. It is amazingly informative for so small and inexpensive a book.

TUNNELS

A History of Tunnels, by Patrick Beaver. Citadel Press, 1973. (ISBN 0-8065-0369-6)
    This is much more than the history of tunnel construction. It gives the major tunnels of the world, with an account of the building of each as well as its length, width and depth below the surface. This part is factual and valuable; the last chapter, though, is a forecast of possible future tunnel constructions and some of these predictions come fairly close to science fiction.

UNIFORMS*
see
ARMED FORCES - GUIDES TO THE MILITARY LIFE

UNITED NATIONS*

Who's Who in the United Nations and Related Agencies.

Arno Press, 1975. (ISBN 0-405-00490-X)
There had not been a new Who's Who in the United
Nations for almost 30 years so this volume fulfills a definite
need. It lists all Secretariat staff members over the rank
of Section Chief, all members of permanent missions, all
members of Executive Boards, members of the International
Court of Justice, retired senior members of the Secretariat,
living past presidents of the Council and many others associated with related agencies. The fly-leaf has an excellent chart
showing interrelationships and a listing of all related agencies.
For each person, the following information is included: name,
positions, address, nationality, languages spoken, date of
birth, marital status, education, publications and honors. It
also gives his/her home phone number.

A Chronology and Fact Book of the United Nations, 1947-1974,
by Waldo Chamberlin, et al. 4th ed. Oceana Publications, 1970. (ISBN 0-379-00189-6)
This overview of the activities of the first 27 years
of United Nations activity provides valuable factual data on
the organization.

UNITED STATES - ATLASES

Index to Maps of the American Revolution in Books and
Periodicals, by David S. Dupy. Greenwood Press, 1974.
(ISBN 0-8371-7582-8)
There are plenty of maps of the actions of the American Revolution but most are not contemporary. In this book
are indexed almost all the copies of original Revolutionary
War maps which have been reproduced either in books or
periodicals. Not only military maps are indexed; there are
many dealing with the civilian life of the time. This book
is likely to be of limited appeal to the smaller library, but
any institution dealing with detailed historical questions will
find it a definite benefit.

National Atlas of the United States. Published by U.S.
Geological Survey. Government Printing Office, 1970.
(I 19.2 N21a)
This is a masterpiece of atlas construction. It was
compiled by the best brains within the government, aided by
the faculty of twenty or more colleges. It contains 756
maps as well as hundreds of insets. It will be of great help

to businessmen engaged in international trade but is equally important to the social scientists. There is a detailed subject index and a locating guide for over 41,000 places. It costs a lot but is worth every cent.

U.S. HISTORY - REVOLUTION

The Bicentennial celebration saw a proliferation of books dealing with the American Revolution. While most were repetitious, some should be in every library and the following are my selections for that honor.

Atlas of the American Revolution, selected and edited by
    Kenneth Nebenzahl. Narrated by Don Higgenbotham.
    Rand McNally, 1974. (ISBN 0-528-83465-7)
    This is an excellent combination of cartographical knowledge and American history. The seventy maps are arranged in chronological order and each is accompanied by comments by Mr. Nebenzahl, on the production of the map, and political and historical comments by Mr. Higgenbotham, who concentrates on the events and leaders of the war. It is more than an atlas, since it lists every unit taking part in each battle. This is a book which should be in every American history collection.

The Encyclopedia of the American Revolution, by Mark Mayo
    Boatner. Bicentennial Edition. McKay, 1974. (ISBN
    0-679-50021-9)
    This compilation by one of the best American military historians covers the period from 1763 to 1783 and is an alphabetical arrangement of the people and events who made the American Revolution. Although all facets of the Revolution are covered, the book is particularly good for biographical information on the political and military leaders of both sides. The book also has excellent cross-references.

An Outline History of the American Revolution, by R. Ernest
    and Trevor Dupuy. Harper & Row, 1975. (ISBN 0-06-
    011127-5)
    Two famous military historians turn their considerable talents to an outline of the American Revolution, with great success. There are good descriptions of individual battles and of all military units, as well as a biographical section on American leaders. Well written, it is one of the best books to come out of the Bicentennial.

People and Events of the American Revolution, by Trevor N.
  Dupuy and Gay M. Hammerman. Bowker, 1974.
  (ISBN 0-8352-0777-3)
   Although there will be criticism of this book because
of its rather meager identification and descriptive passages,
it has many features which cannot be easily located in any
other book. Section one is a day-by-day chronology of the
American Revolution and covers the political, cultural and
military events of the war. The second section is an alphabetical arrangement of the men who made and fought the war.
Although short, the biographies cover almost every major
figure. Particularly interesting is an appendix which lists
persons of importance by their trades or professions.

WATERGATE

   Few events in the history of our country engendered
as much animosity or had a greater effect upon the internal
affairs of this nation as the break-in of the Democratic Head-
quarters in the Watergate Building just prior to the 1972
presidential election. The repercussions from this event
shook not only this country but others as well, so it is not
surprising that there have been a multitude of books on the
subject. Many are valuable for their varied interpretations
of the events; two, however, should be in every library for
research purposes.

Watergate: An Annotated Bibliography, edited by Kenyon C.
  Rosenberg and Judith K. Rosenberg. Libraries Unlimited,
  1975. (ISBN 0-87287-116-9)
   This is a bibliography of periodical articles, newspaper editorials and books dealing with the subject. Since
new books are appearing daily, it should be used only as a
starting point.

Watergate: Chronology of a Crisis, by Editors of Congres-
  sional Quarterly. Congressional Quarterly, 1975.
  (ISBN 0-87187-070-3)
   This covers the chronological development of the
Watergate crisis from the beginning of the Senate Inquiry to
the final pardon of Richard Nixon and the trial of other de-
fendants. The period covered is from April 14, 1973 to
January 4, 1975. It has four parts: Break-in and the Senate
Inquiry, White House Tapes, Impeachment Threats, and Pardon

and Cover-up Trial. This book, compiled from weekly editions of the Congressional Quarterly, is valuable for its presentation of the continuity of the events.

WEATHER*

Weather Almanac, ed. by James A. Ruffner and Frank
    Bair. 2nd ed. Gale Research, 1976. (ISBN 0-8103-
    1043-0)
    This is intended to be a time-saving reference book in the field of weather information and it succeeds admirably. There are eight main sections of the book: U.S. Weather in Atlas Form; Storms and Severe Weather Information; Retirement and Health Weather; Air Pollution; Marine Weather; Be Your Own Forecaster; Record-Setting Weather; and Round-the-World Weather. The information is gathered from various government agencies and is wholly reliable.

WELDING

The Welding Encyclopedia, ed. by T. B. Jefferson. 17th
    ed. Jefferson Publications, 1974.
    Since the Welding Handbook published by the American Welding Society is no longer in print, this is the most complete book available. It deals with such basic subjects as the fundamentals of welding, cuttings, types of welding, i.e., gas, arc and resistance, and the weldability of various metals. It answers most questions likely to arise in this subject area.

Modern Welding, by Andrew D. Althouse, et al. Goodheart,
    1970. (ISBN 0-87006-109-7)
    This is primarily intended as a textbook for high school courses in welding, and gives reliable and easily understood instructions on all types of welding processes. Since it is intended for beginners, there is a great emphasis on safety but it could be used by even experienced hands to better their performance. For the small school or public library, this probably would be more satisfactory than the Jefferson book cited above.

WILDFLOWERS*

Wildflowers of Eastern America, by John E. Klimas and
James A. Cunningham. Knopf, 1974. (ISBN 0-394-
49362-1)

Wildflowers of Western America, by Robert T. and Margaret
C. Orr. Knopf, 1974. (ISBN 0-394-49552-7)
    Although Where to Find What listed the magnificent
six-volume set, Wildflowers of the United States by Rickett,
it was pointed out that it was very expensive and that probably only large libraries could afford it. These two volumes
are not particularly inexpensive and you can buy only the
one for your area if you desire. They are naturally not as
complete as Rickett but each volume describes the plants of
its area with excellent photographs. There is a good section
on how to use the book. For the smaller library, these
two may be the source for many years to come.

WINES

The Concise Atlas of Wine, by Wina Born. Scribner, 1974.
(ISBN 0-684-14661-4)
    This is not a guide to wine and wine use although it
does have sections devoted to the ways to select and enjoy
wine. The prime virtue of the book is its analysis of the
wine-growing regions of the world. For each wine-producing
country there is a description of the types of wine produced
and a map showing the location of each region.

Encyclopedia of Wine, by Frank Shoonmaker. New revised
edition. Hastings House, 1975. (ISBN 0-8038-1925-0)
    This is probably the most comprehensive and highly
regarded book dealing with wine ever written. Two of its
five editions have won the French Wine Book Prize and this
one seems destined to win another. The book is both an
encyclopedia and a dictionary since it gives definitions and
pronunciations of wines and wine related terms as well as a
guide to wine tasting, selection and evaluation. In a country
which is just beginning to truly appreciate wines, this is an
important work.

WOMEN*

The American Woman's Gazetteer, by Lynn Sherr and Jurate
    Kazickas. Bantam, 1976. (ISBN 0-553-01041-7)
        Arranged geographically by state and then alphabetical-
ly within the state, each important landmark in the history of
American women is listed and described, with the reason for
its inclusion given. There is a good name index for finding
individual women.

The Rights of Women: The Basic ACLU Guide to a Woman's
    Rights, by Susan D. Ross. Dutton, 1973. (ISBN 0-87690-
    136-4)
        The American Civil Liberties Union has published a
series of books dealing with civil rights which is intended to
inform Americans of their legal rights. This one deals with
the problems women face in all aspects of American life and
the possible ways of changing them. In the appendices there
are several helpful charts for women needing legal help as
well as listings of women's rights associations.

Women's Rights Almanac, 1974, ed. by Nancy Gager. Eliza-
    beth Cody Stanton Publishing Company, Bethesda, Mary-
    land, 1974.
        This is announced as an annual publication on women's
rights. It is to be hoped that it continues because the first
volume is an excellent beginning. The book is in four sections, each dealing with a specific area of women's rights.
An appendix lists bibliographies and sources of legal aid.

WOODWORKING

An Illustrated Encyclopedia of Woodworking Handtools, In-
    struments and Devices, by Graham Blackburn. Simon
    & Schuster, 1974. (ISBN 0-671-21874-3)
        Once again the subtitle provides an adequate annota-
tion: "Containing a full description of the tools used by
carpenters, joiners and cabinet makers with many examples
of the tools used by other woodworkers such as: woodsmen,
sawyers, coach makers, wheelwrights, shipwrights, wain-
wrights, coopers, turners, pattern makers and whittlers of
various types of tools and instruments used in building and
woodworking." The book is well illustrated and is often

the only place that one can find such tools described.

The Complete Book of Woodworking and Cabinet Making, by
Byron W. Maguire. Reston, 1974. (ISBN 0-87909-153-
3)
    Closely related to the problems of the home repair
man is the question of woodworking and this is an excellent
introduction to the building of cabinets and containers around
the home. It has excellent and well-illustrated instructions
for every step in the building and finishing of the cabinet.
Especially helpful are the tips on shortcuts and the warnings
of things to avoid. It also discusses the types of tools needed
for each type of building. A series of questions at the end
of each chapter allows one to gauge how well he has learned
the things covered in that chapter.

WORLD WAR I

First World War Atlas, compiled by Martin Gilbert. Macmillan, 1970.
    While this includes more than 150 maps, it is really
much more than an atlas. There are biographical sketches
of war leaders and issues to be debated. The primary
value, of course, remains the excellent maps, which cover
every aspect of the war, and the diagrams of important events.
It is well indexed and a worthwhile purchase for any library.

WORLD WAR II

A Biographical Dictionary of World War II, by Christopher
Tunney. St. Martin's Press, 1973.
    Some say that great men make great events, others
that great events make great men. Whatever your belief,
here is a book which should be in any library aiming at
good historical coverage. It is a listing of almost 500 military, political and civilian leaders (including such support
personnel as actors, writers, and others) who were either
heroes or villains during that war. One might quarrel with
the fact that only the war period is covered in the biographies, but it does a good job there.

WRITING*

Forgotten Scripts, by Cyrus H. Gordon. Basic Books, 1968.
  (ISBN 0-465-02483-1)
    This is basically a book about the discovery of ways
to decipher ancient writings and the effect that these discoveries have had on the study of history. There are excellent
pictures and line drawings of various ideograms.

Writing: Man's Great Invention, by J. Hambleton Ober.
  Peabody Institute, 1965. (ISBN 0-8392-1139-2)
    Another excellent history of the development of writing,
with chapters on each of the various forerunners in Mesopo-
tamia, Crete, Egypt, Syria and Greece. A beautiful book
with excellent charts of all types of ideograms.

ZIP CODES

    Each of the major almanacs has a section in which
ZIP codes for the various cities are listed but the Post
Office produces a complete listing by streets for each city
or military post. This is available from the Superintendent
of Documents.

National ZIP Code Directory. U.S. Post Office. Superintendent of Documents. Annual. (P1:10/8)

ZOOLOGY

Collegiate Dictionary of Zoology, by Robert W. Pennak.
  Ronald Press, 1974. (ISBN 0-8260-7100-7)
    This is probably the most comprehensive dictionary
in the field of zoology: 19,000 terms are defined including
technical and common names of various families of animals
and the names of prominent zoologists.